D1348307

YOUR
INNER
COACH

YOUR INNER COACH

A STEP-BY-STEP GUIDE TO INCREASING
PERSONAL FULFILMENT AND EFFECTIVENESS

IAN MCDERMOTT & WENDY JAGO

PIATKUS

Visit the Piatkus website!

Piatkus publishes a wide range of best-selling fiction and non-fiction, including books on health, mind, body & spirit, sex, self-help, cookery, biography and the paranormal.

If you want to:
- read descriptions of our popular titles
- buy our books over the internet
- take advantage of our special offers
- enter our monthly competition
- learn more about your favourite Piatkus authors

VISIT OUR WEBSITE AT: www.piatkus.co.uk

About the authors

IAN MCDERMOTT is a leading trainer, consultant and author in the field of Coaching and Neuro-Linguistic Programming (NLP). In 1988 he founded International Teaching Seminars (ITS). ITS is now Europe's premier NLP coaching and training organisation and has an international network of affiliates. Ian remains Director of Training because he is passionate about training the next generation of NLP Coaches and Practitioners and, through advanced training, providing them with a pathway to personal and professional success.

As a coach and a consultant, he works with many FTSE-100 and Fortune 500 companies, including Coca-Cola, Cable & Wireless and IBM, as well as organisations in the public sector and the BBC. He is the co-author of twelve books on NLP and coaching, and his books have been translated into fifteen languages.

Over the last two decades Ian has trained thousands of people in using the techniques outlined in this book. He now works with some of them in creating new ventures. At present he is working on a couple of new books, projects designed to promote health and well-being, and a new business model which will enable people to determine their personal mission and create wealth by following it.

WENDY JAGO has been learning, teaching and writing about NLP since she first encountered it in the early 1980s. At that time she was working as an Ericksonian hypnotherapist and counsellor, and the elegant and powerful techniques of NLP rapidly became part of her therapeutic repertoire, helping her clients and her professional students grow in their lives and in their work. Her own learning and skills took a similar step forward when she trained with Ian to Master Practitioner level and then became one of the first certificated NLP coaches worldwide. She now coaches both private individuals and senior executives in major international companies.

Wendy has always been inspired by helping people to discover their potential. Having lectured at the Universities of Sussex and Brighton, and worked for twenty years as a therapist, it seemed very natural to use authorship to reach an even wider audience. This is the third book she and Ian have written together, and they have others in preparation.

As a committed dressage rider and judge, Wendy has also pioneered the application of NLP and coaching to issues affecting riders and their horses through her two successful books *Schooling Problems Solved with NLP* and *Solo Schooling*, and through private coaching and master class training.

Contents

Acknowledgements

Finding a way to describe how to engage with what is normally out of your conscious awareness has made this both an exciting and a demanding book to write. For that reason we are more than usually grateful to the editorial team at Piatkus, who have given us their informed and valuable criticism, judicious editing and unflagging support. Our warm thanks to Gill Bailey, Anna Crago and Barbara Kiser.

We would also like to acknowledge the patient yet enthusiastic encouragement of our partners, Paulette and Leo, through the many meetings, drafts and redrafts. They have helped us to articulate our passionate belief in the value of Inner Coaching and to give it shape and structure.

Finally, we would like to express our gratitude to Mark Hewitt, whose readiness to engage with this playful way of working provided the impetus to begin this project in the first place.

The extract on page viii from *The Fifth Discipline* by Peter Senge (Hutchinson, 1993) is used by permission of The Random House Group Limited; the extracts on pages 12 and 159–60 are from *Hare Brain, Tortoise Mind* by Guy Claxton (Fourth Estate, 1998); the extract on page 50 is from *The 20 Minute Break* by Ernest Rossi (Zeig, Tucker & Theisen, Inc, 1991); the extract on page 96 is from *A Wizard of Earthsea* by Ursula Le Guin (Atheneum, 1991); the extract on page 146 from *The 7 Habits of Highly Effective People* by Steven R. Covey (Simon & Schuster, 1999) is used by permission of Simon & Schuster; the extract on pages 148–9 is from A. A. Milne, *Winnie-the-Pooh* (Methuen, 2001); the extract on page 155 is from Charles de Kunffy, *The Ethics and Passion of Dressage* (Half Halt Press, 1994).

Implicit in the practice of personal mastery is another dimension of the mind, the subconscious. It is through the subconscious that all of us deal with complexity. What distinguishes people with high levels of personal mastery is that they have developed a higher level of rapport between their normal awareness and their subconscious. What most of us take for granted and exploit haphazardly, they approach as a discipline.

Peter M. Senge, *The Fifth Discipline*

Introduction

Being in charge of your life means being in charge of yourself. You've probably encountered people who know vast amounts about certain subjects and display great professional expertise, but who seem all over the place as people. Despite their knowledge, they lack that personal mastery.

This mastery is not just worth pursuing: it is the royal road to joy and fulfilment. You can't buy it and you won't find it somewhere out there in the world. The words of Peter Senge, which appear on the opposite page, show us where to look.

Senge makes a number of crucial points that make up the rationale for this book:

1. Everyday conscious thinking is not enough to handle the complexity of our experience.

2. All of us deal with complexity through the subconscious.

3. Some people do regard their subconscious as a valuable personal and professional resource.

4. It is possible to create a higher level of rapport between your normal awareness and your subconscious.

5. People who commit to building such a relationship achieve more – and achieve it more easily – than people who don't.

In this book we want to show you how you can become one of them.

In our work as consultants, therapists, trainers and coaches over many years, we have found that there are certain basic principles which help create and sustain such a productive internal relationship between you and yourself. There are certain assumptions that help; there are certain states of mind and body which make it easier to actively engage in this way, and there are ways of approaching and conversing with yourself which are much more productive than others. These are the keys to success. You can use them to become more personally effective in every arena of your life – for the whole of your life. In this book we want to show you how.

Your unconscious is as much part of you as your eyes, ears or toenails. When we use the word 'unconscious' we're including everything about you that you don't have regular, immediate access to. This includes much about the workings of your body as well as those of your mind. It also includes your ability to surprise yourself and others – as when you wonder, 'Now where did *that* come from?'

Trusting your unconscious is about trusting yourself. Working with your unconscious is about working with yourself. It's the most natural way of being fully integrated in mind, body and spirit. It's discovering that within you there's a source of information, judgement and wisdom. You will find this wisdom within through a process of dynamic inquiry which we call Inner Coaching, and it will give you more riches than you ever imagined possible.

Chapter One

Inner Coaching: a Tool for Life

One of the most exciting and rewarding skills we can learn in life is working with the unconscious. When you 'check in' with yourself regularly and attentively, when you are willing to wonder and be humbled by the amazing power that is yours all the time, when you're prepared to learn from your own inner workings and to make friends with what you can't closely analyse or define – then you open up to yourself a truly remarkable dimension of your own potential.

Building this kind of rapport with yourself, and learning how to make it a regular, automatic and disciplined part of life, will allow you to gain reliable access to incredible resources – and you will also feel more whole and at ease in yourself.

The dimension of mind we're concerned with here goes by many names, and figures in many different kinds of effective work. We choose to refer to it as the *unconscious* or sometimes *the other-than-conscious* because this describes quite literally what we're talking about: those mind-body processes which take place outside conscious awareness.

We fully expect that as you read this book you'll find that some of the experiences we describe are already familiar to you. That's because everyone already has some ways of working with and benefiting from their own unconscious processing. But we know you'll also encounter a lot that is new, because what we're offering is a way of engaging systematically with your unconscious. Only when you know how to do this can you develop reliable personal mastery.

What we're offering doesn't require previous training, because it works with what is already going on within you quite naturally. It offers you effective ways of developing and exploiting this internal connectedness so that you develop a greater confidence in it – and in yourself.

Inside information

Perhaps what happens outside of conscious awareness can't be described in hard-and-fast terms. But a great deal can be deduced about how it works, how it's different from conscious processing, and how it can best be cultivated and drawn on. This book is not about theory, however – it's about what you can actually do.

Most of us are familiar with the concept of coaching. It's a process for helping you achieve what you want. Your goal may be something specific, like a career change. Or it may be something less tangible, like a greater sense of fulfilment. It could involve understanding how you hold yourself back from what you could potentially achieve. It might bring about greater insight, greater confidence or greater effectiveness – or all three. You can be coached by someone else, or you can learn to coach yourself. Overall, coaching is a great tool for development and change and is widely used to help people manage life and work issues more effectively.

But what is *Inner* Coaching – and what is different about it?

Inner Coaching is a powerful process which we have developed. It is a relationship with yourself that allows you to draw on even more of the resources you naturally possess. It gives you access to types of information, mental processing and mind-body connections which generally lie outside the usual scope of life or executive coaching. Much traditional coaching relies on information that's available to your conscious mind and that can be worked with consciously. Inner Coaching assumes that there's a lot more to you – and to effective coaching – than this.

Your emotions, gut feelings, dreams, and the subtle and often neglected language of your body and its reactions are resources that lie within you and are too often ignored or thought to be puzzling, problematic, even mysterious, and out of reach. Inner Coaching helps you access those resources and draw on your full potential.

We've worked with individuals and groups for many years and written several books on coaching and training, as well as on Neuro-

Linguistic Programming, which is the science of personal and inter-personal effectiveness. As trainers, therapists, coaches and writers we've both shared the excitement of helping people learn, grow and change. We have been privileged to touch many thousands of people's lives – each one of them unique. Our experience is that each and every one of us is naturally equipped with an amazing range of capabilities that cross the divisions between what are often thought of as opposites – 'mind' and 'body', 'thought' and 'emotion', 'conscious' and 'unconscious'.

It's clear to us that many of the most effective people we've met, in every sphere of personal and professional life, don't make such rigid distinctions. So, quite naturally, they have access to their less charted inner regions. They have an ease in themselves and in what they do.

For example, we know a businessman who has been really successful in motivating his staff, even during times of downturn, because he instinctively and appropriately draws upon a full range of personal resources: he is warm *and* task-focused, empathic yet direct, down-to-earth but with a strong sense of the more intangible things that matter to people. He is comfortable with elation and anger, anxiety and success, sadness and irreverence – in himself as well as others. We might sum this up by saying that he has naturally cultivated just the kind of inclusive openness to himself that we are talking about. Yet even he, and others who are naturally comfortable with their unconscious processing, could make more of their internal resourcefulness if they knew more about how they do it and were able to use it more deliber-ately and consistently.

However, many people often feel quite alienated from certain parts of themselves. We knew a very talented academic whose specialism was English literature. He analysed, with great sensitivity, how works of liter-ature explore relationships and emotions, but he didn't invest in recognising or working with his own. So when life events really pressed in on him, he didn't have enough emotional flexibility or resilience to cope, and had a serious breakdown.

Social training and formal education do not help us to move natur-ally across the divisions and bring about inner change. We have been taught to rely heavily on a limited range of obvious and easily accessed capabilities, to value them exclusively and to lose confidence in those which are more tenuous, less obviously 'on tap' and less easily 'proved'. You could say that Inner Coaching is a way of rebuilding these inner connections. By working with Inner Coaching, you will have more of *you* available to you – all the time. It will give you a way to restore your ease and enjoyment in living.

The Inner Coaching process is *interactive*. Coaching in all its forms involves a back-and-forth exchange, in which the client is stimulated to clarify, to explore, to discover, to stretch, to build their commitment to themselves and to make changes happen. So it is with Inner Coaching – with an important difference. There isn't *one* part of you which always takes the 'Coach' role. Inner Coaching is both a *state* of enquiry and receptiveness and a *process* of interaction and exchange. It's about attending, giving and receiving – and you play every part. Your Inner Coach is *you* – all of you.

The mind-body connection

During the 20th century our understanding of how the mind and body worked, and of the interconnections between them, was greatly expanded. In fact, psychological and physiological investigations – working, as it were, from opposite ends – began to demonstrate that the commonly accepted distinction between mind and body couldn't really be sustained any longer. There's just too much connection, too much overlap – too much *integration* – between what used to be thought of as distinct entities or specialised systems of functioning.

The Inner Coaching process will help you to use this connectedness of mind and body. It will enable you to cultivate a state of curiosity, receptivity and mindfulness where you can explore the resonance of unconscious processing that occurs through gut feelings, intuition and dreams, or access your memory and creativity more fully and effectively.

When you allow yourself to become reflective and receptive, you can tap into a fuller range of your ways of knowing and being. Your normal frontiers of awareness will become more permeable, so that you receive different kinds of information from within. Becoming receptive like this leads you on to a deep kind of curiosity and exploration. Inner Coaching doesn't necessarily provide you with instant answers. Sometimes it will – just because all you needed to do was come home to yourself to know what was really right for you. At other times, it helps you home in on important questions and discover relevant information which you may have overlooked or didn't realise you had. Either way, it takes you forward.

Inner Coaching helps you become more sensitive to your own inner wisdom, too. Ian often describes this as the 'wisdom within'. As you build the habit of working in this way you'll learn to recognise the confirming signals from within that tell you the answers you're getting are the 'right' ones.

Like conventional coaching, Inner Coaching doesn't have to be a serious business. There's excitement, joy and often playfulness in engaging in this kind of enquiry and discovery. In our experience, play deserves to be taken just as seriously as work in enhancing personal fulfilment and effectiveness. That work/play division is another of those handy yet artificial distinctions which can limit us more than we realise.

We have each been using forms of Inner Coaching to help people for many years. It's only recently that we decided to pool our knowledge, experience and thinking to make Inner Coaching more widely available by outlining what it is and how you can go about doing it. This has involved us in unpacking the beliefs that underlie the process, just as much as formulating the practicalities of how to do it successfully.

This has been a modelling process. That is to say, we have sought out people who are models of excellence and looked in detail at what they actually do. We have also extensively reviewed what it is we have actually done with clients over the years to enable them to develop this skill and then go on without us. We have then distilled the key elements for success. We have found that people who succeed in Inner Coaching share a similar mindset and use similar techniques. We shall therefore focus on both because you need both to succeed.

Modelling excellence in any skill is a key process in Neuro-Linguistic Programming (NLP), which we mentioned above. NLP is a process that underpins much of our coaching work and that we describe in *The NLP Coach*. NLP offers ways of understanding the bedrock principles and processes that underlie the way people think and act. It has generated practical tools for change and achievement in many fields, including education, therapy, business, healthcare, the expressive and performing arts, communications and sports.

This book is not about NLP, yet it rests on the core NLP discovery that the detailed modelling of every aspect of excellence in a behaviour or skill will yield the 'recipe' that enables other people to learn or become better at it. In this sense, our expertise with NLP has given us the tools to describe and share just how the natural process that we call

Inner Coaching works, and how you can use it to enrich your life in very profound and far-reaching ways.

Let's look at what these are.

1. It accesses guidance from within you

Inner Coaching is a collaborative, non-judgemental process, allowing all your abilities and resources to work together, having your well-being as the ultimate goal. You can use your Inner Coaching time to ask for help from parts of yourself outside your current conscious awareness, or you may find such other-than-conscious parts of yourself taking the initiative in alerting you to something useful or even vital for your well-being – whether it's a need, a problem or an asset.

2. It is a reflective process

You can trust Inner Coaching to work for you and with you. It will reflect yourself back to you in ways that are both illuminating and rigorous.

3. It helps you find the right answers

Your Inner Coaching doesn't necessarily give you answers, any more than an external coach would. Instead, it helps you search in the most relevant areas and ask the most productive questions, because coaching takes place largely – and most powerfully – through questions, particularly the kind which prompt you to explore.

4. It enables you to identify your goals

It helps you to discover what you really want, as opposed to what you think you want or feel you ought to want. It will also put you in touch with the powerful mind-body resources you need to foster and it'll maintain the drive and purpose you need to keep yourself on track as you work towards your goals.

5. It is an ongoing inner relationship

To get the most from the practice of Inner Coaching, you will need to make it regular, consistent and ongoing. Like other important relationships, your relationship with all of you needs nurturing, and at times, patience and tolerance.

The benefits of Inner Coaching

Cultivating an Inner Coaching relationship with yourself will give you:

- Much fuller information about your nature, your potential and the way you interact with your world

- Greater access to your own resources – and a new understanding of how extensive they really are

- An increased ability to self-monitor and self-manage

- A greater sense of ease with yourself

- The ability to work towards your chosen goals with a more unified energy and commitment

- More effective strategies for interacting with others

- An enhanced ability to make wise choices and live your life to the full

- A sense of wonder at both who you are and who you might become.

In our experience, the skills that you practise initially through your Inner Coaching become increasingly rapid and automatic, so that you become able to shift quickly and effortlessly between different states of awareness, accessing a fuller range of potential information almost without thinking. And it can all begin naturally, easily and immediately from the very first moment you make the commitment to work with yourself in this way.

Though this process is reflective, it isn't passive or static. Rather, as you actively engage in it, you may feel as though you're making a journey. Maybe at times it will be like taking the Grand Tour, marvelling at strange customs, new experiences, wonderful monuments and artefacts. At other times it may be like following a quest, encountering challenges, disasters and triumphs as you seek your personal goal. Either way, one thing is for sure: there is always more to discover on your unique personal journey.

How to use this book

You'll find that *Your Inner Coach* reflects the nature of these investigations. Sometimes it's very down-to-earth and practical. Sometimes it's speculative, tentative, intuitive, even mystical or spiritual. This is because there's nothing more practical and everyday – *and* nothing more mystical and special – than this amazing process of living your life with the help of your own Inner Coaching.

Each chapter explores a key aspect of the Inner Coaching process. As you read, you'll find simple tips for things to do and to avoid, questions to ask yourself and issues to reflect on. This variety mirrors the variety of your body-mind – and the many different ways in which you can become more aware of its richness, its messages and its potential.

Inner Coaching – first steps

So what exactly do you have to do? The process of Inner Coaching begins with what we call entering a state of mindfulness: that is, one of mild curiosity and attentiveness. It's certainly not just switching off; and it's not disciplined thinking either. In the martial arts you are taught to 'see with soft eyes'. Instead of straining to see you relax, and as you do so you actually observe much more. So it is with Inner Coaching. As the book progresses, we'll be suggesting specific ways in which you can apply this mindfulness. For the moment, though, we'll just describe the process itself. What follows is not a set sequence, but rather guidelines that we've found helpful for starting off. Read our suggestions through, and then let yourself follow the spirit of them rather than the letter. With practice, you'll find what works best for you.

▶ Allow yourself some time to yourself – anything up to 20 minutes will do. As you get more used to the process, you'll begin to find that you can sometimes pose a question, raise an issue, start a search or even receive an answer in much less than this. Like any skill, the process of Inner Coaching becomes smoother and more natural the more you practise it.

▶ At first you may want to make sure you will not be disturbed, and that you're physically comfortable. If you're sitting down, we suggest that you sit with your hands on your lap or on your knees and both feet flat on the floor. (If you have your arms or legs crossed you can get pins and needles after a while, which will interrupt what you're doing.)

▶ You could let your eyes close, if that feels natural, or just stare off into space without focusing on anything. You want to turn your attention inwards, rather than allowing external things to distract you.

▶ As you get used to paying attention to your inner experience, you'll find you can switch into this state pretty much anywhere. You may, for instance, prefer to do it when out walking with your eyes wide open. What remains the same is that you're checking in with yourself. So stop trying and just be with yourself.

▶ If you have a question, or a concern, that you'd like to work on, allow it to rise into your awareness. Don't start earnestly cogitating. Instead relax into it. Just let it be in your awareness.

▶ Because you're tapping into areas of yourself that are outside your conscious awareness, you don't need to do anything else – in fact, you really need to learn to *do nothing* other than be curious about what may begin to happen.

▶ Accept that questions may spark off other questions; that answers may come in puzzling forms rather than as straightforward replies; that your thoughts may wander; that you may even feel as though you fell asleep briefly. You process in many different ways.

▶ If you find your mind wandering, that's fine. Inner Coaching doesn't require concentration or deliberate thought – only a willingness to be available to whatever comes.

▶ If your thoughts start racing, you might like to remind yourself that you can deal with whatever-it-is later. Right now, you need to be available to yourself. Perhaps you might like to imagine a space waiting to be filled, a sheet of paper waiting for a word or a phrase, a listening ear waiting for a sound ... or some other idea that suggests anticipation followed by arrival.

▶ At some point within your 20 minutes, you'll probably start to feel as though you're reconnecting with everyday thoughts and feelings again. This may happen after you've become aware of some thought, question or idea, or without anything seeming to have occurred at all.

▶ Trust the process: in our experience, you have set things moving even if you don't as yet have any clear signs, and this is probably why you've begun to feel reconnected with the everyday world again. So just go with the change in your state and get on with whatever comes next in your day.

▶ But be prepared to be receptive, for the effects of an Inner Coaching relationship with yourself, like those of external coaching, often come after the event ...

Wisdom comes to those who are willing to expand their sense of themselves beyond the sphere of conscious control to include another centre of cognition to which consciousness has no access, and over which there seems to be little intentional jurisdiction. As Emerson puts it: 'A man finds out that there is somewhat in him that knows more than he does. Then he comes presently to the curious question, Who's who? Which of these two is really me? The one that knows more or the one that knows less: the little fellow or the big fellow?'

Guy Claxton, *Hare Brain, Tortoise Mind*

Chapter Two

Your Amazing Potential

Think of yourself as a person who has a vast wealth of knowledge and ability within you. But suppose you don't *know* you possess this hidden wealth or don't know *how* you can reach it?

There are everyday clues to the presence of this interior treasury all around us. Our gut feelings, or the stories we're drawn to, are just two examples. Yet often these clues have become so familiar that we discount them, and the guidance they can offer is lost. Think of the very phrases and idiomatic metaphors of our language, or the myths and legends of older civilisations: they have much to tell us – if only we would listen. This wisdom is both within and around us.

You are the most exciting, mysterious, complex, resourceful being in the known universe. We're going to show you how Inner Coaching can help you to discover the hidden riches within you – even though you may not think you know exactly what they are or where they are to be found. By monitoring your own intuitive responses as you explore you will receive the feedback – which is such a critical part of good coaching – that tells you when you are getting closer or further away in your search. In this sense you *do* know your inner potential at some level already. But in following the straightforward suggestions and exercises in this book, you'll become more confident, more relaxed and much more playful. You'll get to enjoy becoming aware of yourself and exploring, trusting and enriching yourself. And this book is going to show you how.

There's a children's game generally known as Hunt the Thimble. It has many other names and variations, but the basic idea remains the same. A player nominated as 'It' leaves the room and is blindfolded while the other players hide an object – originally a thimble – somewhere. When 'It' returns and begins to search, the others call out 'cold', 'hot', 'cooler' and 'warmer' in response to how close the searcher is getting.

Our 'gut feelings' can operate in a very similar way if we let them, because they can get us an intuitive, fuller range of information on which to base our decisions. People who ignore these feelings because they can't offer a logical explanation for their hunches often live to regret it.

Another example of natural wisdom is that of mythology and our responses to it. All civilisations have their myths and legends, telling the stories of ancient heroes and heroines. At the core of these stories there is usually a basic dilemma or quest: the problem and its resolution are often exemplars of patterns that recur in human life, reaching beyond the specifics of the time, place and culture in which the tale is set. We often find ourselves attracted to particular myths or popular stories: paying attention to them and teasing out what they mean to us can often help us better understand what we are dealing with right now in our lives.

Sometimes we surprise ourselves by what we can do in a tight situation. 'I didn't know I had it in me,' you might say. A young mother whose child has become trapped under a car simply lifts the car so that the child can crawl out. How does someone who weighs less than 130 pounds lift a car weighing half a ton? And some years ago an agricultural worker had his arm severed when his tractor overbalanced on a slope and fell against him. He picked the arm up and walked a mile for help, feeling no pain. How did he manage this miraculous feat? These are amazing testimonials to human resourcefulness.

At the other extreme are the kinds of skills that come into play in everyday life. To those who possess them, they are quite unremarkable. But to others, they are a source of curiosity, even envy.

Wendy's mother often forgot to wear a watch, because she always knew what time it was – to the minute. How did she do that? Winston Churchill was renowned for being able to take ten-minute catnaps wherever he was, which may have been critical in helping him survive the long years of war. What was it that enabled him to do that? We have a friend who went on a course on basic computing. She was immediately able to replicate all the procedures that had been demonstrated without hesitation and without further help. How did she do that?

Someone else we know discovered in his forties that he was allergic to dairy products and had an underactive thyroid – yet he had always hated milk and cheese and ever since his teens had drunk large amounts of coffee. He had instinctively avoided the dairy products (which could have set off an allergic response), and compensated for his low metabolic rate by stimulating it with caffeine. He didn't *know* that he was tuning into his body's aversions and needs, but 'just felt more comfortable that way'.

These are the everyday miracles that a person is likely to take quite for granted until they realise that other people don't seem to have the same gift. They usually don't know what makes it possible for them. The skill operates unconsciously.

Our experience is that we all have gifts like these, even if we are not aware of them – and that there are many more awaiting our discovery. We have so many billions of brain cells, with so many possible connections between them, that we can never exhaust what might be. Habit and training and life experience make certain connections familiar, and every use of those familiar neural pathways makes them seem more and more inevitable, even fixed. Yet when you allow yourself to consider that what's familiar to you about yourself is only a fraction of what you might be able to think and feel and do, you create a 'willing suspension of disbelief' that allows you to transcend your own limitations. And in this state of openness, Inner Coaching gives you the perfect vehicle for new links to be made, weak links to be strengthened, old limitations to be dismantled and hitherto undiscovered or overlooked resources to become available.

Connecting with your inner resources

What kinds of inner resources are we talking about? We can think consciously – and process unconsciously. We are both logical and poetic. We have amazing minds and wonderfully complex bodies – and the two can communicate brilliantly and effectively with each other in ways that science is only just beginning to understand. We have memory and imagination. We can recreate experiences in our minds with stunning special effects, including full technicolour, sound and physical sensation. This can make us feel elated or, depending on the content, prove sickening, depressing and very scary. We sort and categorise according to a range of specialist systems, and make amazing leaps of creativity that go beyond the limits of what we know logically. We dream. We can watch a suspense movie and as the excitement builds, so our heart rate soars.

All these wonderful capabilities are at our disposal – yet all too often our access to them seems random, or can be blocked. And perhaps even more often, it's underestimated. In our work as coaches and trainers we have found that many people may be ready to accept that other people are amazing – 'But not me. There's nothing extraordinary about me.' But there is.

What happens when you take notice? – and what happens when you don't? What happens if you start from here? If you don't look, you won't find. If you aren't expecting, you won't notice. And if you don't notice, you won't be aware of the promptings from within – for every part of yourself can teach you something, give you some benefit or help you realise your potential more fully. And so the miracles they can deliver won't proliferate.

We want to shake up this thinking. We're inviting you to make the daring assumption that you too are amazing, and then to begin to notice just *how*. And the more you notice, the more you begin to discover. There's a whole world of wonder in *you*. It's like gaining access to a well that's inexhaustible, to a storehouse of power that's limitless. The more you dip in the more the water refills, because as you dip in and draw on it you stimulate it at its source. The power is limitless not because you can do everything but because you can usually do *something* – and almost always more than you might have expected. This is the nature of the wisdom you have within.

The map and the territory

So the first step is to give yourself permission to presume more about yourself. If you look at a map, you know that it isn't the actual territory it represents. However useful a guide it may be to finding your way around, there are plenty of things it doesn't tell you. How things smell on a damp autumn day. How vividly green things can be when the sky is covered by black thunderclouds. How much sound there always is. How the air tastes. How grass cushions, how pavement resists, how mud sucks.

That is the territory. What each of us knows about our own body-mind is at best rather like the map – a navigational aid but so much less rich than the real thing. Yet people tend to operate as if their individual maps actually are the reality – and so the map they have in their minds ends up shaping the reality they experience. This goes for maps of the self, as well. When you think of yourself as having certain skills, or personal qualities – or, conversely, as lacking them – you're referring to the map you have of yourself. And each time you do this you make your reality more like the map.

Inner Coaching gives you a valuable way to explore just how your map of you may help you in life, and to discover just how you could add to it to make life richer. It's a bit like the old maps with *here be dragons* written in the corners, or people's lack of geographical knowledge making them assume the existence of the North West Passage, or that if you sailed west you would come directly to China. Inner Coaching helps you gain more information precisely because it helps you hold some of your limiting territorial assumptions in suspension so that you can wonder, explore and discover more ...

Maps do have their uses though. Just as you can use the map to find your way around in the landscape, you can use what you already know about your own self as a basis for the most exciting kind of travelling any of us can do: you can identify your path and follow it more purpose-fully, and you can explore and become familiar with territory that is at present unfamiliar, even though it belongs to you.

A large part of your interior territory will be unfamiliar because it's outside your conscious awareness. There can be two reasons for this. The first is because you currently aren't paying attention to certain aspects of your experience – for example, your gut feelings, or your dreams, both of which come into consciousness but are not created by it. The second reason is that some parts of this interior territory are less imme-diately available to you: it's as if there's a screen between you and, say, your memory storage or many of your physiological processes. But even these can become more accessible to you, as you discover the unique channels that link the conscious 'you' to them and learn to connect with them.

You and yourself

During the course of this book we'll be guiding you in your internal exploring and helping you to enhance your connection with yourself. Sometimes we'll say 'yourself' rather than use words like 'subconscious' or 'unconscious' because these are already linked with particular systems of thinking about people and how they function – and because 'yourself' includes your whole complex of mind-body connections. Coaching is based on a relationship – and in this case we suggest the relationship that needs cultivating is between you and yourself.

Listening to the message

What happens when you start thinking of yourself as a unified whole, made up of many mutually interconnecting systems? We've found that this can be profoundly liberating, because it frees you to acknowledge and benefit from *all that you are*. Becoming aware of the many possible links there may be between the different levels on which you function and between different parts – for example, between thinking and feeling, between what you're experiencing in your body and how you're feeling emotionally – helps you become increasingly alert to more and more subtle ways of receiving information from within. As you do this you become able to enrich your experience of living.

What sorts of things might you begin to discover? Well, you might find that the uneasy feeling you have in your stomach on Sunday nights is warning you that the job you once enjoyed is becoming too stressful. You're uneasy because you and the job no longer 'fit' together. Or you might still believe that the job is a good one for you, yet feel you're not being stretched by it any more. Why worry? You can do it easily, and there's plenty of energy left over for other things. It seems silly to quit – doesn't it? Yet you want more.

You might allow yourself to recognise that the hesitancy you feel when an old friend asks for a simple favour is a sign that somewhere inside you've started to notice that the favours have all been going one way without a sign of payback. There's no particular reason to refuse any of them, but somehow the friendship isn't equal any more. Often people feel guilty in these kinds of situations, and try to convince them-selves that they shouldn't complain, or that it's wrong to be dissatisfied when things are good enough. Yet if you attend to your inner wisdom alerting you via these intuitive signals, you really know that you should make changes. That's what the dissatisfaction, or the headaches, or the unease, has been trying to tell you.

It isn't wrong to feel dissatisfied when you think you 'really ought' to feel that things are good enough. You simply want more. It's natural, and when we coach people we encourage them to reach for the maximum. This is not about being ungrateful for what life has offered you, or being greedy, or in some way being selfish when you know that so many other people out there have a much harder time and 'real' problems to contend with. It is positive, and it is a way to grow.

Feeling obscurely ill at ease and trying to ignore this tentative signal is much more of a problem. Why? Because ignoring your inner prompt-ings disconnects you from yourself – and when you're disconnected you become progressively less able to sense what is really right for you. Ultimately, you may end up becoming physically or emotionally ill because you haven't listened and made changes at a point when it would have been easier. Conversely, the better you get at hearing your inner wisdom when it whispers – rather than only when it shouts – the smaller the corrections you'll need to make to keep yourself on course. So this is about becoming receptive to yourself.

How do you get access to yourself?

It's really very simple. There are two things you need to do.

1. Allow yourself to presume that there is more to discover, to achieve and to enjoy

Think of the map and the territory again: if you confine yourself to the bit of the world you already know, you may never go beyond its bound-aries. Even if it's pleasant and satisfying, you'll never know that there was more to know, more to find out, more to do. You're missing out. Perhaps even more importantly, you're missing out on having the *choice*.

2. Pay attention to what your senses are telling you

All day, every day, information is available to you through your five senses: seeing, hearing, touch, smell and taste. Through habit, you have learnt to pay more attention to some kinds of information than others. Some people 'live in their heads' and don't notice what their bodies are experiencing. They watch the world instead of feeling a physical part of it and connecting with the people, things and events that are going on within it. Some people feel a lot but don't notice what they're seeing. Some people only 'hear' the content of what's said to them, not the way it's said. Even within the senses you favour, you're likely to have blind-and-deaf spots. Life experience, education and social training have taught you that some things are 'more important' to pay attention to than others.

If you're to connect with yourself and access the wisdom within you, you need to give yourself time – and permission – to notice things as fully, freshly and without filters as you did when you were a child. A recent TV sitcom, *Third Rock from the Sun*, concerned a group of aliens who arrived on Earth as research scientists, assuming the appearance and roles of human beings in order to do so. But of course they didn't share our unquestioned 'knowledge' about what things mean and how things are done, so they made 'mistakes'. Their inappropriate reactions and naive responses gave watchers a commentary on what we take for granted as 'normal' behaviour. That was what made the programme funny. Seeing your own world with a fresh eye can be just as intriguing.

Perception operates through filters, and filters become habits. When Wendy's daughter Charlotte was little, she was fascinated by buttons and began to collect them. Wendy and her husband learnt to walk the streets scanning the pavements for buttons to take home to Charlotte – and it was amazing how every walk, however brief, produced two or three. The world is full of dropped buttons – if you are looking for buttons! What if you are looking for friendship? or new opportunities? or things to amuse you? or kindness? or a chance to be helpful? or puzzles to solve? The world is full of them. And what if you are looking for new ways to realise the potential that is in you? Opportunities abound – but *only* when you start to look for them.

Tuning in

As we explained in the last chapter, Inner Coaching begins with enter-ing a state of mindfulness or inner attentiveness. One specific benefit you can derive from it is to connect more fully with your mind-body information. In order to do this you can learn a simple, three-stage process that we call tuning in.

1. Make yourself available to your experience

To start with, you may find that it's easiest to first put yourself into a mindful state in the way we described earlier, on page 10. Then check out the kind of information each of your senses is giving you. To do this, you need to set aside learnt patterns of 'ignoring' discomfort or illness. Instead, you need to progressively cultivate your ability to notice and discriminate between different kinds of sensory information, and allow yourself to engage with your senses, recognising them as significant bearers of information from the internal as well as the external world.

We receive information through our senses, but we also use them internally to replay past events, manage the present or imagine the future. So they aren't just receivers – they are also transmitters, sifting information into 'familiar' and 'strange', 'safe' and 'dangerous', 'pleasant' and 'unpleasant'. What you receive as information – particularly if you aren't really paying attention – has already been highly edited. Ask six people who were present during the 'same' conversation what they heard, and you'll get six different versions. Your ears, your eyes and your physical sensations will all have contributed to what you actually noticed. Change the balance between them and the re-edited version will suddenly create a very different experience, which may even be more useful or enriching to you. Learning how to tune in takes time at first, but the more of a habit it becomes, the easier it gets – and the more extensive and reliable the information you can draw upon.

2. Learn to recognise your own signalling system

Recognise your patterns. Do you get sick feelings, or headaches, when things aren't quite right? Do you perhaps become restless and itchy? Do you feel bouncy and full of energy when something good is in the offing, or perhaps instead experience a quiet sense of peace? Learn to pay attention and to understand these messages and what they mean for you. If you act on such a feeling, does it diminish? or does it become stronger?

3. Learn to notice smaller and subtler distinctions

When you become aware of differences and changes, you will learn to fine-tune the messages. This kind of fine-tuning, or calibration, gives you the precise kind of information you need to guide you in your quest.

For example, a friend of ours began to notice that he often felt slightly irritable and mildly off-colour at weekends. He didn't know why this might be, but he'd often found that taking time to tune in gave him useful information. So he started to tune in on Fridays and monitor his energy level and sense of well-being, establishing a benchmark for a 'normal' or acceptable state. Once he'd done this, it became clearer that by about Saturday afternoon he was feeling more sluggish physically yet also more agitated mentally. He felt much the same all weekend, but by mid-afternoon on Monday he was feeling 'himself' again.

He took himself into a mindful state and asked himself a really good Inner Coaching question: *'What's going on?'* And the answer came immediately, *'Bread'*. During the week he just had an egg for breakfast, and soup and salad for lunch, no bread. But on Saturdays he had more time, so he had toast, and often bread and cheese for lunch. Tuning in allowed him to identify bread as the trigger for his slight mood change. Then he became aware of other patterns indicating that his body was mildly intolerant of wheat. Now he understood! After that it was simple to find wheat-free but enjoyable foods he could eat at weekends, so that he could remain 'himself' all the time.

Building a habit

How do you get into the habit of attending to yourself, and really listening? Almost certainly not by telling yourself it's something you ought to do. How many other 'oughts' become joyless chores that you somehow never quite find the time for? If you exhort or badger yourself to do something, your heart isn't really in it: your head has made a decision which you're trying to impose on yourself. When you connect with yourself through Inner Coaching, it doesn't mean you have a licence to order yourself about.

Think for a moment about something you find truly easy to do regularly. Our guess is that it's either an emotionally neutral, long-established, automatic pattern, or else one that you really enjoy because your heart *is* in it. We want tuning in to be something like this. Your heart and your head both need to be in it.

So how do you find time and space in your busy life for another pattern? Simply identify circumstances that would make it natural and easy, and then arrange to put yourself in those circumstances, or notice when you already are. In the television series *Faking It,* a young female kick-boxer had the task of learning in a month how to pass herself off as a skilled Latin-American dancer. She was given training by skilled and experienced coaches, but found it impossible to let herself relax and become physically expressive. However much her trainers showed her, exhorted and bullied her, she remained physically wooden and emotionally uninvolved. The breakthrough came when she was sent on a day's improvisation workshop. Here, she and the other participants were asked to do things like crawl around and over each other on the floor, or run about and shout. It was ridiculous, but everyone was doing it together. No one looked stupid. She began to enjoy it – and after that she found it much easier to become expressive in her dancing.

How did the improvisation teacher make the magic happen? He'd put her in circumstances which made it impossible *not* to behave in the way that was wanted. It was a laugh. Everyone was busy doing it themselves. Even she wasn't watching herself critically any more. *It was easy and natural.*

When you're building the skill of tuning in to yourself, take advantage of anything that makes it easy and natural. When you're driving along a familiar road and your mind wanders, notice how easy it's been to hop, skip and jump from one idea to another, or to dream or reflect. When you're standing in the shower remembering the date you had last night, or imagining how today might go, be curious about just *how* you are doing that. Are you running a movie in your head? Are you telling yourself a story? Do you get a tingling in your toes, or a prickle at the back of your neck? At times like these you're already on your own wavelength – just pay yourself the extra compliment of noticing what wavelength it is. This is one natural and immediate way of learning and promoting Inner Coaching: paying attention to the information you are giving yourself and just how you are giving it, and allowing yourself to wonder what it's telling you and how you could benefit.

So you have two ways to connect with yourself. You can choose to connect with yourself deliberately when you want to or need to by being mindful and tuning in. And you can also utilise 'accidental' or naturally occurring moments.

How do you know you're connecting with yourself?

When we try something new we want evidence that something different is happening. That's natural. And the evidence is there – when you attend to it. Connecting with yourself through Inner Coaching is a different kind of 'knowing' from the one we're used to most of the time.

Usually, you'll be aware of feeling different, or being in a different kind of state. (There's more about states later on.) You may have a sense of being 'spaced out', or of time passing much more slowly, or much faster than usual – perhaps a feeling of time*less*ness. You may feel slightly disconnected from the outside world for those moments when you're tuned in to yourself. You might feel cooler, or warmer, than you usually do. You may find that ideas, or solutions, or other thoughts just 'arrive' in your mind without your first being aware of a train of thinking leading up to them. This is because you're processing more information than you could possibly handle at a conscious level, or even than you'd consciously think was relevant. This is why we know how powerful gut feelings are, yet can so easily persuade ourselves to disregard them: they don't come with their 'workings' tidily visible.

In the chapters that follow we're going to guide you on what we believe could be the most exciting and productive journey of exploration anyone could undertake. It's a journey that can help you achieve your specific goals, yet takes you further than any one of them. It's a journey into unknown territory that turns out to be astonishingly and comfortingly familiar – and still remains mind-blowingly exciting. It's a voyage that begins and continues through connecting with the wisdom within *you*.

So how is being in touch with yourself through Inner Coaching going to benefit you?

When you acknowledge messages from within – even if you decide not to act on them – you're likely to feel more at one with yourself at every level. In NLP coaching, we often refer to this sense of personal harmony, when everything seems to be flowing together, as 'congruence'.

Inner Coaching can help you put your immediate concerns into a bigger picture or a larger time-frame. The benefit of this is that this may take some of the sting out of them, put them in a different perspective or allow you to see where you are headed. When you have a sense of the bigger picture you can see things from a range of different perspectives, and so find it easier to tolerate, or even welcome, things that you'd normally think of as antipathetic in some way. This may give you a richer understanding of others, or of other parts of yourself. To be able to tolerate paradox is to experience life in a different way.

Where you are still discussing something with yourself, you may find yourself paradoxically enjoying the sense of interplay you get between the different parts of yourself. Even where important issues are involved, the debate is dynamic and productive, without conflict. This feeling of 'oneness' is likely to be reflected in increased physical comfort. For example, you may notice a feeling of relaxation, your breathing may slow down or your shoulders may lose their tension. You may feel suddenly at peace – and you'll feel all of a piece. You will have a strong sense of being whole.

Above all, you will achieve a sense of balance. Balance is a word that's often misused to mean a static state in which one thing virtually cancels out its opposite. This is not what we mean. Balance is not stasis. Think about riding a bicycle, or walking. Both involve continual adjustment if you are to remain in balance. They involve activity that is dynamic and fluid. That's what life requires of us: a continual adjusting. We might call it evolution – that's what is involved when you connect with the wisdom you already have within you.

INNER COACHING EXERCISE: PAYING ATTENTION TO YOU

While getting started requires nothing but your attention, paying attention in an open, wondering way is a skill that needs to be learnt. Follow the pattern we outlined in Chapter 1 to get yourself into the right frame of mind and body, and use some of these simple suggestions to begin exploring:

▶ Take a few moments to consider the amazing complexity and wonder of your body. Do something simple like turn your hand over. How did you do that?

▶ Take a favourite memory and allow yourself to recall it through all five of your senses, remembering what you saw, heard, felt, perhaps even smelt and tasted. Did you find extra details coming back to you?

▶ Think of a time when you surprised yourself. It might have been something quite small. Perhaps no one ever knew about it but you. What was the event, or the thought – and just what did it tell you about *you*?

▶ Think of some times when others surprised you by their resourcefulness, insight or humour. How does this round out the impression you have of them?

Chapter Three

Approaching Your Inner World

What could be more familiar to you than yourself – and yet how often are you puzzled by the way you think, or baffled by what you seem driven to do? Sometimes you can feel that your own impulses or thoughts are as alien as if they belonged to a stranger. Or you can know that a particular behaviour you have is unproductive or even self-sabotaging – yet you seem unable to change it. Even beneficial aspects of yourself, like your moments of inspiration or talent, may seem to appear from nowhere. Yet it's a nowhere that's inside you and part of you!

While some people are relaxed about 'not knowing' themselves, others find it disconcerting, even at times alarming, to sense such a discrepancy between the self they know and can monitor consciously and the parts of the self that function outside their awareness. In our experience, Inner Coaching gives you a way to become more at ease and more familiar with *all* of yourself, even though much of your physical and mental functioning will forever take place at other than conscious levels. That's why we've called this chapter 'Approaching Your Inner World'. Some areas of the interior will always remain inaccessible – and indeed that's how they naturally work. But you can certainly get to know more about them and what goes on there, and you can become more comfortable about 'not knowing'.

Exploring you

Inner Coaching is both a state and a process, and in this chapter we're going to outline some key ways you can make both easier for yourself. Like any country, your inner world can close its borders or ensure that you don't get very far inside. But if you approach it in the right way, your explorations, and your ability to discover more, can become natural, enjoyable and productive.

In working with many different people in a variety of therapeutic, training and coaching contexts we have often heard people talking about what they themselves feel or how they think with as little understanding as if they were talking about a total stranger. Sometimes they feel baffled, sometimes helpless. Yet with appropriate guidance you can learn how to build familiarity and a good working relationship with every part of yourself. If you learn even a little of the customs and language of these less familiar parts of you, you have much more meaningful and productive inner communication.

Just as in foreign travel, many of the delights of inner exploration are in the small, unexpected incidents and perceptions: seeing new sights, hearing different sounds, experiencing new sensations, realising that even without words you have made yourself understood. Have you ever pretended you are on holiday in your own home town? When you look at it with a visitor's eyes, there seems to be so much more to notice. It's as though you're sensitised to things you'd normally overlook. How could you possibly have missed them before? The difference lies in how aware and how receptive you are.

Getting to know yourself better is very like this. Being open in this new way involves two things: curiosity and acceptance. You need curiosity to drive your travels, and acceptance to ensure that you don't rush to premature judgements about what's useful, important or valuable. Only with a kind of wondering acceptance will you be able to discover what any unfamiliar land has to offer you – and that includes your own interior.

Once you have established this attitude of wondering acceptance towards yourself – including those parts that feel strangest and most 'foreign' even to you – you are in a position to enter into a fruitful relationship with them. This attitude is the foundation for Inner Coaching, and enables you to increasingly benefit from your own inner wisdom and resourcefulness. At first you may not even know how to make the most of your own newly discovered qualities and abilities – a bit like the impoverished husband in a famous *Punch* cartoon who looks at his newly acquired bathtub and says to his wife: 'Nice little barf, Liza. Wot shall we do with it?' It can take time, sensitivity and experimentation to find out.

One example is when you feel at odds with yourself. For example, your logic may be telling you that you really should give up smoking, or change your job, or get out of that damaging relationship. But this potentially helpful advice may be quite insignificant or even valueless as far as your emotions are concerned. *Your heart isn't in it.* Adding more logical reasons won't make it any easier to act sensibly, because your heart doesn't talk that language anyway. All that happens is that the louder your logic shouts, the more your heart gets deafened and upset. The conflict escalates, and each side of you trusts the other even less. You need to improve the relationship.

Building a different kind of relationship with yourself can actually be very straightforward. We will show you how to navigate with more confidence in this inner world, to negotiate successfully between different needs and impulses and to gain access to some of the riches which were actually yours all the time.

Jenny was married to a head teacher, and very much caught up in the life of his village school. When he suddenly died from a heart attack, she was lost. For years she had gladly invested all her energy – even her very identity – in her marriage and her role as the head teacher's wife. Now she was bereaved in every sense. Everything seemed meaningless and empty.

One day a friend insisted that Jenny went with her to a local art exhibition, and Jenny's eye was drawn to some examples of calligraphy. Something in her told her to take a close look, and then to get information about classes. Because Jenny had learnt Inner Coaching, she took this impulse seriously and followed it up. Tentatively at first, Jenny went along and tried – and as she developed her new skill she found she was also discovering a real talent, and a new Jenny. Her sense of loss still took its own time to heal, but a new purpose did come into her life as she first planned, then wrote out, a book of quotations on bereavement in her beautiful Italic script. This was published, and became the first of a series in which she was able to offer consolation and hope to many people through her new skill as a calligrapher and designer.

Jenny had never thought of herself as a designer, and before her bereavement would never have dreamed of wanting or finding a new sense of identity – though she instinctively took the opportunity when it arrived. For her, the shock and dislocation of bereavement reminded her of the need to do some Inner Coaching; and her receptiveness to her own inner promptings then allowed her undiscovered potential to grow. But of course you don't need disasters like this to create the opportunity. From time to time it can be really enabling to use your Inner Coaching time to wonder about what more you might be capable of … and how you would find out.

Primarily, approaching the inner world is about changing your focus of attention. You need to learn how to disengage from the busy world of external stimuli and to become attentive to those signals coming from within. In Chapter 4, we'll talk you through a number of straightforward and simple ways of doing this, each of which helps you to change from one kind of state of mind-body awareness – the everyday one you're used to – to a more specialised one that helps you reflect and receive information from within. But before you can learn to pay attention to something different, or pay attention in a new way, there are several essential conditions to fulfil.

The four keys to entering your inner world

There are four vital keys to entering your inner world, and you need them all:

1. A willingness to attend to information from all your senses

2. The right attitude and assumptions

3. Consideration towards yourself

4. A willingness to check out in advance the possible implications and consequences – for you – of what you want to achieve.

Key 1. Tuning in to information from all your senses

In the last chapter we gave you a brief introduction to tuning in, a vital tool in Inner Coaching. Now we need to explore how you can broaden and refine that core process so you can get the most value from it.

Potentially, you have access to many different kinds of information about yourself. You have your five senses: sight, hearing, touch/feeling, smell and taste. However, most people tend to pay more attention to some senses than others.

Some people have actually learnt to tune out important information from their bodies and about their feelings; others have learnt to follow their feelings and tune out their logic. Some tuning out is inevitable: in order to avoid being overwhelmed, we have to be selective about what information we attend to. This selection can be influenced by upbringing, life experience and education, and the information that does get through may be heavily or inappropriately skewed.

The problem is not that you tune some things out: it's that you get used to a particular *kind* of tuning out. So you get gaps in the information available to you. A particular kind of tuning out may have been natural at one time in your life, but it will also be limiting. Later it becomes a habit. For example, some people who survive unpleasant physical experiences instinctively learn to desensitise themselves to physical sensations. They tune out their kinaesthetic channel. This may have once had immense value as a survival tactic, but it also means that subtle signals which may be helpful just don't get through, and pain or illness may have to get quite severe before they notice and can attend to it.

This is what happened in Sophie's case. She had had a hard childhood, though she couldn't remember much about it. One effect seemed to be that she found it really difficult to tune into what was going on in her body, and tended to push herself very hard physically. It was only when she had a serious illness in her fifties that she realised how distant she felt from her physical self, and perhaps how that might have come about. She decided she really didn't want to 'dig deep' and try to find out more about the origins of this pattern – what she called 'living in the safety of my head'; but she did promise herself that she would learn to connect more with her body and look after it better in future.

You need to get to know what's missing and what your individual blind spots and black holes are. Take a moment to ask yourself the following questions:

- Which of your senses would you say you attend to most naturally?

- Do you rely heavily on one or more of these senses?

- Do you tend to ignore other senses, or notice them only when the signals become really strong?

- Do you find it difficult to pay attention to any particular source of sensory information?

INNER COACHING EXERCISE: SENSING YOURSELF

Like Sophie, you could set about retraining yourself, so as to even out your availability across a fuller range of information. Here are some ways you could do this:

▶ Think of something you enjoy doing. Notice *how* you are thinking of it. Are you picturing it, feeling what it's like, hearing how it goes? Now think of it again, but this time ask yourself what other information is available – perhaps sounds or smells. If none come to mind, what ones might be present? Can you add them in now?

▶ Imagine something you'd enjoy in the future. Notice how you naturally run your scenario, then add in more sensory dimensions.

▶ Next time you do something pleasant, make a point of gathering information across a broad range. Walk 50 yards paying attention to smells. How many? How do they change? What are they? Stop and shut your eyes – how many different sounds can you hear? Look at a leaf or a lawn: how many different shades of green can you see?

▶ Do something you really enjoy – and this time pay really close attention to every detail of it.

One summer, some friends of ours had been for an evening meal at a restaurant by the sea. When the meal was over, it was late and the moon was rising. The tide was at its lowest, and the family decided to walk along the beach. Because the sand was wet, they took their shoes off – and immediately a whole world of sensations opened up to them. They found themselves noticing tiny changes not only in the degree of wetness but in the density of the sand, its relative hardness, crispness and ability to withstand weight. Playing with these differences, they tuned in to smaller and finer distinctions, zigzagging back and forth from the sea's edge. They amazed themselves – and created a memorable experience which they talked about as a family for years afterwards.

What fine details and differences could you notice as you relive your chosen experience?

Whether or not you are consciously aware of your sensory process-ing, it's always going on. Sometimes this means that you receive the results of your own processing without the 'evidence' that supports them. We'd urge you to take these rapid impressions and gut feelings seriously, and in fact we explore the latter more fully in Chapter 11. For now, however, we just want to make the point that instant impressions like these can be a really valuable source of information.

If you'd like to regain this skill, play with it. Guess the weight of the cake – literally. Guess how many pigeons there are around that old lady as she feeds them, and so on.

A friend of ours has a version of this game. When she and her husband bought their first set of bathroom scales, she began to guess her own weight before stepping on the scales. She was amazed to find she was right. Having tried this the first time for fun, she has gone on 'guess-ing' on a daily basis as a way of reinforcing and continuing to marvel at this wholly unconscious ability. She is rarely out by more than a pound – and then mostly when she thinks about it a few seconds too long and tries to take information (for example, recent eating and exercise patterns) consciously into account. Her conscious mind just hasn't got the same ability.

Key 2. Your attitudes and assumptions

In any relationship, what you assume about someone else can influence or even determine what kind of relationship with them is possible. What you expect may well be what you get. This is because your beliefs influence what you say and do and how you respond, so that they shape what is possible for the other person. Your body language, your tone of voice and how you 'hear' and interpret their actions, will all be influenced – perhaps critically – by what you assume about them to begin with. The same process applies when you encounter new customs, a new country or a new activity. How you approach them will have a substantial effect on what you find. Neutral or positive assumptions will tend to help you get the most from other people, situations or countries – and the same thing applies with the assumptions you make about yourself.

We've found that some assumptions in particular can be really enabling in making contact and forging relationships. If you want to approach other parts of yourself and your less-familiar functioning more closely, you're more likely to succeed and benefit from what *every* part of yourself has to offer if you start out in the right way.

Here are some guidelines we've found useful in helping people to approach their inner worlds.

1. Assume even parts of you that feel in conflict, or unhelpful, or that are outside your conscious awareness, have an attitude of goodwill towards you as a whole

Obviously, not everyone out there wishes you well – but if you behave as though they did, the majority of people will not disappoint you. You will be sending them signals of trust at many levels, and a belief in trustworthiness tends to produce trustworthy behaviour. This doesn't mean you should blind yourself to contrary evidence, or that you shouldn't evaluate the responses you get. But it's a better basis for dialogue than suspicion or cynicism.

You can use the same principle to enhance your inner life. If you assume that your gut feelings are intended to give you useful – even vital – information, that your dreams are helpful ways of processing your experience and could help you, and that even your 'bad' habits seek (or sought in the past) to achieve something of value for you, then you not only put yourself in a position to receive and benefit from that information but also lay a foundation of trust between the different dimensions of yourself.

This means being willing to take a new look at any of your feelings or behaviour that cause you problems. It also means being prepared to trust yourself when you make a snap judgement, or have a strong sense of intuition about something. You may not be able to account for such things logically, but presuming some kind of positive intention behind such less easily explained phenomena invariably reveals new information that helps make sense of what's going on. The atmosphere of goodwill which this creates makes it easier to build fruitful relationships internally. So consider:

- What assumptions do you currently make about parts of yourself you know less well or feel less comfortable with?

- If you did presume their goodwill towards 'you', what would change?

2. Presume that you're intelligent

People often say, 'It's stupid of me, I know, but I can't help . . .' This kind of critical self-judgement compounds any existing sense of self-alienation, and doesn't take things forward at all. Mostly, it makes you feel even worse, since in addition to doing, thinking or feeling whatever it is you can't stop, you feel stupid because you can't.

Assume instead that the bit of you which is responsible is in its own way as intelligent as you. Start wondering just what kind of (good) reasons it might have for being or behaving like this. This approach seems to have the effect of unifying you with a part of yourself you were looking down on, or even wanting to cut off from, beforehand.

Here are some examples from our clients:

- 'I know it's silly, but I just can't stop smoking.' (In fact he found the unconscious purpose was to give himself small rewards and to make regular pause-breaks during hectic days at work.)

- 'I feel so stupid, but often when I'm in a relationship I can't stop myself from asking my partner if he really loves me. It's been the reason for a number of break-ups, actually.' (The self-caring intention was to protect her from investing too much in a relationship that might not last.)

> ### INNER COACHING EXERCISE: LEARNING FROM PROBLEMS
>
> Coaching isn't always a comfortable process – but there's often valuable information to be found when you pay respectful and non-judgemental attention to things you find puzzling, problematic, stupid or even shaming about yourself.
>
> ▶ Take one of your attitudes, behaviours or habits that you tend to think of as 'silly' or 'stupid'. If it were actually an intelligent response to something, what might that be? What might that tell you – about the pattern, about your life, and about you?

3. Assume that you are worthy of respect

Maybe your life is a mess, you made mistakes you regret, you have habits you dislike, and you feel incapable of changing. There are, in short, parts of you that you don't respect. Now ask yourself whether you would do your best for someone who didn't respect you. Well, then, why would you expect a despised or undervalued part of yourself to be cooperative with anyone – like you – who fails to value it?

Lucy collected ornaments. At one point she found herself thinking, *'It's simply stupid of me to keep on collecting all these ornaments. I've even got three the same. How idiotic can you get?'* But at the next sale she saw another example and couldn't resist it. Was she being stupid – or was it just that her rational, logical mind didn't understand and so couldn't begin to appreciate that a different kind of motivation might be involved?

What we are talking about here is the kind of relationship you have with yourself, and how it can be improved so that it can become the most valuable, sustaining, exciting and fulfilling relationship you have in your life. Without respect, it's not worth having a relationship. But whereas you can make choices about the other relationships you have in your life, the only real choice you have about the relationship you have with yourself is to put up with how it is, or to make it better, and better yet.

The payoffs are immense: peace of mind, enjoying your own company, becoming more resourceful and more fun to be with, becoming more trusting and more trustworthy, exploring your own inner country, discovering your own inner resources and riches and bringing so much more to the relationships in your life. Thinking of every part of yourself as a potential friend is a great way of developing this most important of all relationships – the one with yourself.

Talking with a friend one day about her collecting habit, Lucy said casually: 'Of course, I didn't even have my own room when I was a child, and so I couldn't have my own things.' It was as if she had heard herself for the first time. 'I think I'm beginning to realise why it's so important for me to be able to collect things of my own now that I'm grown-up,' she said in amazement. This was the start of an important journey of exploration for Lucy. She no longer felt stupid.

- What do you currently find difficult to respect in yourself?

- If you thought of this as the best response you could make in the circumstances (now or at the time the pattern started), how would your attitude change?

4. Assume that the different parts of you desire to communicate

There's an episode of *Star Trek: The Next Generation* in which Captain Picard is marooned on an empty planet with a representative of another culture with whom the Federation has been seeking to negotiate. Though they speak the same words, they do not understand each other's meanings, for the way they use language is very different. They are frustrated and angry with the situation, with each other and with themselves. Both men know that the key to their survival and that of their civilisations rests with them: they must learn to understand each other. Yet it seems impossible.

Because he presumes that the alien leader bears goodwill towards him, Picard doesn't dismiss or ignore him but instead pays careful attention to what he says and just how he says it. He begins to realise that the other man's every sentence, every reply, alludes to some ancient event or story from his culture's past. It is only by listening carefully, noticing the patterns, and registering how they are used as responses to what he himself says that Picard realises this, and is then in a position to begin replying appropriately – at first tentatively, then with increasing confidence. He literally learns to talk the other man's language. So the deadlock is broken, and the two men face the immediate danger of their isolated situation together. A channel for communication between their peoples has been created.

The same is true for each of us. Without developing ways of communicating between the different parts of ourselves, we are less than we could be and may even be at odds with ourselves. If we take the approach that each part of us desires to communicate, we can work towards a genuine dialogue. We can develop the channels that are needed and ensure that they are monitored. And as we do so, the flow of information between the different parts of us becomes more free, more open and more mutual.

INNER COACHING EXERCISE: EASING COMMUNICATION

▶ Take a part of yourself you find difficult to communicate with. Consider, what kind of language is it using to communicate with you?

▶ Is there a way you could begin to learn and use this language in response?

5. Accept that the 'same' words could well have different meanings for different internal 'users'

As the *Star Trek* story illustrates, it's important to recognise that the same words will not necessarily have the same meaning to different parts of yourself. The technical and logical language of your rational mind, the associative and poetic language of your creative mind, the literal understanding of your unconscious and the metaphoric richness of conscious speech may all share words in common, yet the rafts of meaning they convey can be very different and even at times contradictory. In developing your inner connection, you develop your ability to pay attention simultaneously to many levels of possible meaning.

INNER COACHING EXERCISE: WHAT'S THE STORY?

You can try this out for yourself. Think of a story that really catches your imagination. It might be a television series, a book, a myth, a poem or a film. Now consider:

▶ What is it about it that really gets to you?

▶ What does this tell you about yourself?

An example of how this resonance between individual and story works concerns two people we know. They were each fascinated by the story of Sir Ernest Shackleton, the great explorer, yet it had different meanings for each of them.

Jim had been an impressionable youngster at the time of Shackleton's epic journey across South Georgia, and for the rest of his life venerated Shackleton for the way he had led his men in impossible conditions – and because 'he brought them all back'. As a teenager, he became a Scout leader, and as a young man worked his way through university to become a minister. He saw his own mission in life as that of supporting and nurturing his congregation – in his case, not through ice and mountainous terrain, but through the hardships of the Second World War. His London church became a haven offering shelter, food and community spirit to neighbourhood people who were bombed out and bereaved. Shackleton's inspirational leadership, tempered with hard work, humour and personal faith, gave him the model he and his congregation needed.

Two generations on, Shackleton's story inspired Jim's granddaughter in her turn as she looked for purpose and tested herself against the intellectual and personal challenges of her life. She was fascinated by accounts of endurance and personal heroism, enjoyed strenuous physical sports and had both an admiration and, as an only child, an instinctive understanding for those who by accident or choice managed extreme challenges alone.

The same story meant different things to Jim and his granddaughter. Myths have their own potency to inspire and guide us, whether or not we recognise just how they do this. Yet when we stop to examine just why it is *this* story that grabs us so, and recognise its symbolic role in our own lives, we may be able to gain even more.

Different accounts of Shackleton have explored the qualities that went to make him such an effective leader of men. Becoming aware of the patterns of 'Shackleton's way' can help other leaders to model his behaviour more effectively, because more accurately. We may recognise that sometimes the apparently mundane hardships of everyday life can pose desperate challenges and call forth astonishing acts of leadership, stoicism or courage. And if we're getting bogged down in the mundane, such tales enable us to restore our sense of what it means to be human to a more appropriately heroic scale.

6. Presume each part has a contribution to make

Probably we all have some parts of ourselves that make us uncomfortable. A common response is to deny or try to suppress them, while feeling guilty or even ashamed. Much better, though, to assume that they are attempting to fulfil a valid function for us, and to seek to discover what it is.

Let's take one example. As a professional 'helper', Wendy used to feel uncomfortable that in her 'off-duty' life she would sometimes make rapid and dismissive judgements about people. Once she recognised it, she christened this part of herself 'Hanging Judge'. She didn't like it much. It didn't seem to fit with the faith she felt in people's essential worth.

We all make negative snap judgements from time to time. And so it has been throughout human history, whether it's the Roman crowd baying for blood in the Coliseum, or the milder contemporary version of voting contestants off reality TV shows. There are times when we will feel guilty about some of our more hasty judgements – as when we realise later that we seriously misjudged someone. However, if you just dismiss snap judgements in yourself or others you miss an important point: in real life they can have a protective function.

This was true for Wendy. One day she realised that Hanging Judge could be very useful to her: it protected her from involvement with people who might be unreliable or difficult in some way. On reflection, Hanging Judge was usually right; the problem was that the reasons for these snap judgements only became apparent some time – often a long time – after the judgement itself had been delivered. Once she realised this, Wendy became a lot happier about this 'negative' part of herself, and took the verdicts as useful warnings of the need to be careful and look more closely.

Other things that people commonly dismiss or judge harshly in themselves include behaviour patterns they can't seem to change, and ways of thinking or reacting that seem inappropriate or cause embarrassment (such as feeling 'too emotional', blushing or being afraid of things that other people take in their stride).

▶ Do you have a pattern or a specialised part like Hanging Judge that makes you uncomfortable with yourself?

▶ Do you have a name for it? What difference does it make if you give it a name? And if you change that name?

▶ Do you have a pattern of behaviour, feeling or thought that you feel uncomfortable about but can't seem to change?

▶ How might it be trying to serve your best interests?

7. Presume each bit of you needs contact but may not know that it wants it

As human beings, we are made up of many interconnecting systems. If we are to enjoy good health and a sense of well-being, these need to be in balance. Perhaps it's because of this that we have so many phrases in everyday speech which point to the importance of 'balance', 'wholeness', 'being at one with yourself'. You've doubtless had the experience of feeling 'out of sorts' or 'not all of a piece', or that something is 'off'.

You may say that while 'part of me wants this, another part of me wants that'. On the other hand, you may praise someone for their 'integrity'. There seems to be a strong impulse in human beings to value wholeness and connectedness.

While some organs or parts of the body come in pairs, and some are versatile in the way they function, there's almost no true redundancy in the human system's design. Just about each and every part has a function. Our view is that this is true at every level. Why dream if dreams aren't valuable? Why have an imagination if it hasn't a role to play in your life? If one solution will do, why have the creative ability to think of several? These abilities are part of the human package. If you don't honour and use them you don't connect fully with all that you can be or all of who you are. And if you try to ignore one or other of these inner functions they may have to shout louder, or compete for space and attention instead of working cooperatively as part of the whole of you.

INNER COACHING EXERCISE: ONLY CONNECT

You need each and every bit of you: your Inner Coaching will help you find ways to build greater internal connectedness, and the proof of its value is how you feel when the harmony that comes with fluent internal communication has been restored.

▶ Take a moment to enter a state of mindfulness, and check with yourself which parts of you feel least 'heard'.

▶ How could you become more aware of their messages and more receptive to them? Why not start now?

---

7. Don't rush to make negative judgements about yourself – instead, start to become curious

When we pass judgement on something, we cease to gain new information about it. That's what judgement means – it's drawing a line with a plus or minus to it. So when we pass judgement on ourselves – good as well as bad – we stop the process of enquiry, perhaps temporarily, but often for a long time.

One of our clients remembers being brought up to think it was impolite to drink out of bottles in public. Since it was important to her to be thought of as polite and well-mannered, she avoided drinking out of bottles. It was only when she was in her forties that she thought to ask her mother what had been the reasoning behind the prohibition – and was stunned when her mother answered that it was to prevent the possibility of being injured if a bottle broke!

INNER COACHING EXERCISE: JUST ASK

In our experience, you get a lot further if you let the jury stay out and keep asking questions. Questions get you more information.

▶ Identify some aspect of yourself that you are inclined to judge harshly.

▶ Ask yourself, *'What's that about?'*

Key 3. Mind your manners

The baseline here can be summed up in a simple adage, *Do to yourself as you would be done by*. Politeness and good manners get you further with yourself because they are a way of demonstrating self-respect. If you are courteous in the way you approach yourself, you'll find your inner world much easier to access. If you imagine how you might feel if someone else ordered you about, or asked you to do them a favour and then failed to say thank you, you'll get some idea of what we mean. Even the most remote parts of you have the same sensitivity, as our Inner Coaching clients have found over and over again.

1. Be courteous

Teaching these skills over the years has made it very clear to us that the people whose inner journeyings are most productive are those who take the trouble to extend the same kind of courtesy to themselves as they do to others whom they wish to get on with. Ordering yourself about is likely to produce a stroppy, sullen or switched-off response. After all, why would you let a bossy outsider into your private world? Why would you bother to put yourself out to help someone who was rude or disrespectful?

▶ When you enter into a mindful state, begin whatever work you have in mind respectfully and, if you are using words in your approach to yourself, make sure you are as polite with yourself as you'd be with anyone you regarded highly.

2. Allow time for response

You know that if you want to remember a name or telephone number and find you can't, there's no point in worrying away at it. The age-old cure is to do something else – then the information will arrive of its own accord. Sometimes you'll need to take the same approach when you want to use this unconscious processing to find a solution to a problem, take a new and creative approach to something, or work out why you are behaving in a certain way. Sometimes the answer you seek may arrive hours or even days later when you are thinking about something entirely different. In a way, this is your proof that your inner wisdom was responsible. After all, your conscious mind was busy doing something else!

▶ If you want to test this out, keep a notebook. Jot down what you were thinking of and aiming for – and date it. And then date when you got your answer, or your result.

3. Build trust over small things before asking for big ones

If you are following our guidelines in your approach to yourself, you will be building trust from within the 'you' that's doing the asking. Trust is a two-way process. Often, it's more difficult to build trust the other way – from the logical, conscious part of yourself to your body or the other than conscious parts of your mind. Just as it takes time to get to know a stranger and to feel able to trust them, it may take time for you to trust your own process.

Make the process easy for yourself by getting help with small things first. That way, you'll build a body of small successes which will give you the confidence when you want help over something big. Whether it's to do with remembering information, getting yourself to do something you've been putting off, managing something you find alarming or difficult or managing discomfort or pain, go for the small things first. Trust – and confidence – come with practice.

— INNER COACHING EXERCISE: TRUST YOURSELF —

Here are some possible small things to start you off.

▶ When you go to bed, set your 'internal alarm' by thinking for a few moments of the time you'd like to wake up. It may help to glance at the time it is when you do this, because this can help your inner alarm know the interval of elapsed time that will be involved. As a way to help you relax and sleep normally, set your alarm clock too – but for five or ten minutes after the internal time you've set. That way, you know you're covered – and you have enough time to find out that you can do it all by yourself first!

▶ If there's something you'd like to do later in the day, pause for a few moments, stare into space or shut your eyes and imagine yourself doing it. Imagine yourself 'just remembering' it's time to make that phone call or whatever.

▶ If you have a headache, ask yourself if there's something it's trying to tell you. If you get an answer, respect it. Take some action now on the basis of what it's telling you, or if you can't right now, be clear when you will. *Don't dismiss the information, however strange or unexpected – or even unwelcome – it may seem.* If there's no 'message', you may get a feeling of blankness. No harm, you've checked. Respect the signal value of the symptom. Taking painkillers just suppresses it without gaining the information, which may need to recur, or try other ways to make itself felt.

▶ If you have a symptom that tells you you need professional help, arrange the help. Make the appointment. *Then* remind yourself that you've respected the signal; you've taken action; maybe the signal could now become less intense? Your body-mind will be much more inclined to help you diminish pain signals if it knows you can be trusted to take whatever practical actions are needed. If you don't take action, you will be trying to con yourself – and that can really throw up the barriers between you and your inner world.

A friend of ours had bad toothache – on a Friday just as he was about to go away for the weekend. He made an appointment with the dentist for the Monday. Then he had a conversation with himself. Help was at hand, so the signal wasn't needed anymore. And he had looked forward to this weekend away for quite a while. It would be a pity to spoil it by being in pain all the time. Could something be done to lessen the pain, or make it more distant in some way, given that the cause was going to be addressed in two days? What happened was that though the pain was still there whenever he remembered to think about it, he found himself rather distant from it for most of the weekend, so he was able to enjoy himself. Perhaps not as fully as if he'd not had anything wrong, but certainly more than he'd expected. In fact, he was surprised by how he'd only taken one painkiller. And on Monday, the dentist fixed the problem.

4. Do something every day that helps build your confidence in you

The more you build your self-respect and your self-trust, the more you respect and trust yourself. It's like building muscle. One guiding principle is to ask for things you can deliver, and to reward yourself when you do. This is the foundation for the big ones. Don't take yourself for granted. These are amazing abilities you have; enjoy them and marvel at them and develop them at the pace that's right for you.

▶ Think back over the past week. In what ways have you benefited from your inner resources and abilities?

▶ Take a moment to thank yourself, and to feel that sense of gratitude and recognition.

5. Avoid overload

It can be so exciting to discover these abilities that you can get into overload. It's a bit like asking a helpful friend to get just one more thing from the shops. 'Oh, and while you're there ...' Be restrained!

▶ Prioritise – just as you would with a friend whose good nature you don't want to abuse.

Key 4. Check your ecology

We have got used to thinking of ecology as an external issue; we know about the knock-on effects of environmental change and accidental pollution. We also have an internal ecology that can be preserved, polluted or upset in similar ways. When we are exploring our own inner dimension, we need to be careful about what we find there, and to be attentive to any signals that indicate we may be upsetting the relationships that exist within our own internal systems. This is particularly the case when we seek to make changes. One guideline is to recognise that some kind of balance already exists, and that there can be knock-on effects that reach beyond the immediate change we may be wanting. So it's useful to ask yourself questions like: *'What's the function of how things are at the moment?'* (even things that seem irrational or self-limiting); or *'If I get the change I want, what might be the knock-on effects?'*

INNER COACHING TIPS: PERSONAL ECOLOGY

Some guidelines here are to:

▶ Pay particular attention to new evidence or information that seems to run counter to what you are accustomed to thinking about yourself and the way you work. What you take for granted about yourself may now need updating. Someone we knew thought of herself for years as 'a slow learner', because that was how teachers thought of her at school. It was only when she was in her thirties that she realised she was actually very fast at learning information or skills that *interested* her.

▶ Be curious when something 'doesn't work' or doesn't happen. Consider the positive intent of how things are currently – and the possible negative effects of what you were seeking. Your inner wisdom may already know about these and be holding the status quo to protect you – or to serve some other beneficent purpose. We've known many people successfully use Inner Coaching to help them lose weight. And we've also know some whose weight remained stubbornly the same – because there were good internal reasons which they were unaware of or ignoring.

▶ Experiment with different ways of formulating what you seek, in case there's an underlying problem that stops you from achieving it, or the wording is not completely clear. Just as you can make embarrassing mistakes when talking a foreign language because you don't know the local idiom, so you can inadvertently approach your inner self in the 'wrong' way and have your approach blocked. Keep your language – even to yourself – unambiguous and simple.

In the end, the baseline of all these dos and don'ts is one of respectful curiosity and a willingness to be flexible. Respect, because every part of you, however puzzling or frustrating, is worthy of your respect; curiosity because enquiry gets you much further than judgement; and flexibility because a readiness to try something different and experiment with new customs and different approaches is much more likely to help you on your journey than sticking obstinately to what you know and can do already. Respect, curiosity and flexibility are invaluable to travellers abroad. And they are the foundation of all worthwhile conversations – including those you hold with yourself in your Inner Coaching.

Chapter Four

Getting in the Right State

L ike everything else in life, Inner Coaching is easiest and most effective when you're in the right state for it. As you followed our instructions for becoming mindful and for tuning in, you may have noticed changes in how you felt. Perhaps your body became stiller; your heart rate may have slowed, or you may have felt more relaxed or more centred. Or maybe you felt yourself beginning to focus in more. These differences signal a change in your state – one which happens quite naturally as you shift your awareness.

During any one day, we will move through any number of different states, often without realising it. But what, precisely, is a state?

What states are

A state is simply how your mind and body are at any one time. Sometimes a particular state is so distinct that we label it: excitement, joy, anxiety, fear, relief, worry. But these are at the extremes. We spend more of our time somewhere along the continuum in between the extremes, where states subtly slide into each other like the gradations of light you get with a dimmer switch.

When we label a state it's usually for its emotional component, as in the examples above. But there's a physical component, too. Tension or relaxation, slowness or rapidity of movement, posture, muscle tone, rate of heartbeat and many less obvious things are all involved.

As the everyday phrases 'being in a state' or 'getting in the right state' imply, a state has a profound impact on what's possible then and there for you. Your state affects not just how you feel now, but how you think and what you are capable of doing. This is why states matter for Inner Coaching.

Beginning a journey into your inner dimension, whether it's reflective or explosively joyful, whether it lasts for seconds, minutes or even hours, can be so much easier if you're in the right state. You don't just have to wait for that magically 'right' state to come along. If you learn how to recognise your states and what triggers or facilitates them, you will be in a position to put yourself into the state that's most helpful for what you want, whether it's a state of concentration when you need to work on something, a state of playfulness and enjoyment when you're spending time with friends, or a state for your Inner Coaching.

Some changes in our states occur naturally. Your body-mind has its own recurring rhythms of alternating states. During the course of the day, we go from a state of resting and sleeping to one of activity, and back again. But within the daily period of wakefulness, we experience a number of less obvious cycles of rest and activity. These are known as ultradian cycles, and occur about every hour and a half. Learning to work with them can make many tasks much easier and more 'natural' to perform.

The American psychotherapist and researcher Ernest Rossi found scientific evidence indicating that we naturally alternate from a state of activity and engagement to one of thoughtfulness and greater stillness every 90 minutes throughout the day, and also during the night, when we alternate between periods of deep sleep and those of the more shallow REM, or dream, sleep. Taking this rhythm, and the corresponding way in which people seemed to become more inward and reflective in what he called the 'troughs', Rossi began to help his clients make deliberate use of these times for introspection, inner questioning and healing. There's a strong probability that because the electrical frequency of the brain changes according to what it's doing, it slows down in these ultradian 'troughs' and produces the brain waves known as alpha waves. These slow-wave patterns are a characteristic of states of inner focus: they seem to facilitate the kind of inner availability and inner work we have been looking at.

The beauty of using these naturally occurring breaks in your day for your Inner Coaching is that all you have to do is notice and work with the pattern as it occurs. A senior business executive we were coaching was concerned because his sleep patterns had begun to deteriorate. When we got him to talk us through his 'normal' daily pattern, it soon became obvious that like the majority of his colleagues, he was ignoring any indications of troughs and attempting to maintain the same driven efficiency throughout the working day. After a long day and only a brief evening reconnecting with his family, he was somehow expecting himself to be able to go to sleep just as if he had turned off a switch.

Deconstructing this stressful pattern began with very simple steps: he agreed to take a short walk at lunchtime instead of eating at his desk; to tell his secretary to leave short breaks between meetings; to use unexpected 'gaps' not to catch up on his mountain of e-mails, but to stretch, have a glass of water or even gaze out of the window as he reflected on the needs and happenings of the day; and in general, to pay more attention and respect to the signals of pressure his body was trying to give him. By allowing himself a little more time to unwind he actually helped himself become more flexible – and paradoxically, more efficient.

If the pressure is getting to you, you could take a deliberate break like our client does. And you could also train yourself to notice and respect those moments when you find your attention wandering, or when you begin to stare off into space ... If you learn to spot these signs of a natural trough in one of the ultradian cycles, you can hijack them for some brief yet very effective moments of Inner Coaching.

> *We all work better and more efficiently when we are not fighting our natural mind-body rhythms ... Maximum performance rests on this simple dictum: 'peak your peaks and trough your troughs' ... Peaks are for good outer performance; troughs are for good inner healing and inspiration.*
>
> Ernest Rossi, *The 20-Minute Break*

As well as changing naturally through our daily and ultradian cycles, states can be triggered by external signals, events or places, and by internal stimuli such as memories, fantasies and thoughts. Certain situations, like birthdays, interviews or parties, may recall a state which you've previously learnt to associate with them. The thought of Christmas approaching, for example, calls up many contrasting states: it makes some people feel good as they anticipate shared festivities and being together with those they love; for others, it signals a state of anxiety and weariness as they think of all the work involved; for still others, it's a state of loneliness, dread or misery as they anticipate solitude or remember past trauma. The very word 'Christmas' can be enough to call up intense feelings and old patterns of behaviour for many people.

Many people have discovered special patterns that help them trigger the right state for inner work. Ian meditates every morning and evening, and finds new ideas, new possibilities, and new connections occurring during this time of quiet, internal focus. For him as for many others, meditation melts the normal boundaries of mind and body and disman-tles some of the tramlines of familiar thinking. What seemed like a problem before he started is often seen in a new light. It's a kind of consideration that allows deeper creativity and exploration to occur.

Other people find their innermost wisdom in similar ways through yoga, relaxation techniques such as self-hypnosis or the martial arts. All these involve a disciplined focus which is paradoxically freeing. And there's a willingness to set aside the familiar patterns of logical, conscious thought and rational problem-solving. In fact, this kind of work doesn't involve focusing on problems at all. The state in itself is what's aimed at – and that willingness to be in suspension is what opens up the possibility of so much else.

How do changes in state come about? You could think of your brain essentially as a communications system. Consciously, it tends to link things together in logical sequences and categories. Unconsciously, it connects things through their associations – which is why something like a particular smell or melody can call up feelings and vivid mem-ories. Unconscious linking is like a parcelling up of many things that just happened to coincide. This is why you might have an illogical aver-sion to a particular food because the last time you ate it you quarrelled with a friend or partner, or a feeling of confidence when you wear a particular outfit because you wore it for a successful interview or won the match you were playing. Any detail that was stored unconsciously as part of the experience can call up the whole. It can recreate the state. Knowing this allows you to become alert for what triggers the states you find enabling, and those you find limiting – for anything you have in mind.

Recognising your states

Some states can really make your inner wisdom effortlessly available, and others can block your ability to connect with yourself. Each of us has potential access to a repertoire of many different states: knowing more about how to create and change them gives us the 'open sesame' we need to explore the riches of our own inner world.

You'll certainly be able to recognise the major states you get into – though sometimes you're so busy enjoying or hating the state you're in that you don't think about it at the time, or realise that it's something you can prolong, or change. You are less likely to pick up on states that are less extreme or shifts that are subtle rather than clear-cut – yet these are often the ones that can make Inner Coaching possible, sometimes just for moments or in the most unlikely places.

The pattern for becoming mindful that we showed you in Chapter 1 gives you a way of changing your state to one that facilitates inner exploration, but it requires space, time and a degree of privacy. Once you get familiar with your states and are able to take advantage of them or change them, you can do your Inner Coaching almost anywhere, and take advantage of moments rather than needing minutes. Think of making a telephone call: you could enjoy a lengthy discussion, or you could give or receive important information in a couple of sentences. Inner Coaching is much the same. The essential thing is to be able to make the connection. And the key to that is being in the right state.

There isn't just one right state, because everyone is different. And in order to find your right state – for Inner Coaching or any other activity you have in mind – you first need to get familiar with monitoring your states and state changes.

States affect both how we interpret our experience and what we are able to do about it. But if a state is habitual, how do we get to recognise it, never mind alter it? One simple way is to begin to notice when your state changes for any reason, and to ask yourself what the change tells you about the state you have changed *from*.

Pinpointing a habitual state

You could begin by thinking about the last time you felt surprised by feeling different. What exactly was involved?

- Did your mood change? To what? From what? Perhaps you started the day feeling cheerful, but somewhere along the line you noticed that that feeling of well-being had evaporated. Backtrack – just when did the change happen? Was it sudden or gradual? Can you identify what triggered it?

- Were you aware of different sensations in your body – if so, what and where? Maybe you felt physically warm – then became cooler. Or perhaps you started out relaxed, and then noticed your shoulders had become tense.

- Did your posture or actions change in any way? Did you sit up, stand straighter, or relax, or slump? Did your movements become quicker, or slower?

- Did your thinking change? Did it become more disciplined, or more discursive and free-floating? Was there a change from words to pictures, or feelings?

- Were you more or less aware of yourself in relation to others? Did you feel more outwardly connected, or more inwardly focused?

What you are doing is building a profile of the state from which you changed. If it feels strange to be thinking about yourself like this, think of the last time you had a cold or flu. Monitoring your physical state quite naturally – and probably very rapidly – alerted you to a sense that something was 'not quite right'. What were the first things you noticed? Did you wake up in the morning feeling different, or did you begin to notice changes as the day went on? Were they gradual, or sudden? We all have the ability to monitor state changes, but whereas you may be relatively quick at noticing the onset of minor illness, you may not notice other state changes so quickly or distinctly.

- Now go back to the state you've been thinking about. Was it one you have often been in? Is it perhaps a habitual, or baseline, state for you?

We think of some people as 'cheerful' and others as 'serious'. Labels like these seem to imply that the quality is a fixed characteristic. If you start thinking of it as a *state* that's *habitual* to that person, it begins to seem more accessible – and if need be, more flexible – once you know what the elements are and how they can be triggered.

Ian once worked with a client called Tim, who felt panicky in confined spaces. Tim wanted to change this. Something made Ian ask Tim how it would be if he no longer felt so anxious on the Tube or on planes. There was a long pause, then came an unexpected response: 'If I did change, I don't know how I'd be. It would be like being someone else.' Tim had got so used to his anxiety state that it felt normal: the thought of any change for the better was quite disconcerting. 'It would just be so different ... I'd be so different.' It was as if not only his emotions but his very identity was involved. Only when he'd got comfortable with the prospect of being so different was he ready to change his habitual state for good.

INNER COACHING EXERCISE: THE STATE YOU'RE IN

▶ As you go through today, check in with yourself from time to time to discover what kind of a state you are in. How many states do you experience today? Are they contrasting, or rather similar? Which one(s) would you say are pretty characteristic of you? Are they enabling or limiting in what they make you feel, think and do?

'Right' and 'wrong' states for Inner Coaching

We've explained how some naturally occurring states, such as ultradian dips, can facilitate Inner Coaching. And we've shown how some specific mind-body disciplines can work in a similar way. Before outlining some simple steps you can take to create the right state for your Inner Coaching, we'd like you to know about the things that can get in your way.

What might be the wrong state to begin exploring your inner dimension? If you are overwhelmed by having too many things to do, by acute time pressure, by anxiety or by the need to complete a complex task, you will be in the wrong state for Inner Coaching. Remember what it's like standing in a busy place waiting for a friend to arrive? There is incessant movement, so much going on that you can feel dizzy. Your eyes are darting here and there looking for your friend. It's as if your attention is all out there. Do this for long enough and it becomes a real strain. You can feel agitated, even nauseous, because you can't process so much at once. And after all that your friend has to tap you on the shoulder to get your attention; you didn't see them arrive because you were too busy looking and straining.

You need to have space, and be receptive. It doesn't necessarily take much time though, as we'll show later in this chapter.

Inner journeying is like exploring: you need to be available in mind and body. You need energy; you need freedom to be curious and to notice things as you explore. You need to be alert for new discoveries, and for dangers and distractions. Any state which prevents you from being aware of your inner promptings, that clouds your judgement or narrows your focus so that you discount or fail to notice certain areas of information, is the 'wrong' kind of state.

It can be easy to notice these 'wrong' states when they are triggered suddenly: you open a letter that contains bad news and all of a sudden you switch from your usual cheerful self to feeling helpless and sad. You hit a problem with something you are working on and you don't know how to fix it; suddenly you feel incompetent. Something you had looked forward to is cancelled and you feel unutterably disappointed. In those first moments after your state has changed, the new feeling seems to take you over entirely, perhaps to the point of paralysing your ability to feel or do anything to change things. Your own resources of experience, adaptability, hope, creativity, even logic simply aren't available to you. You're disempowered. You're in the wrong state.

And as we've seen above, you may have developed the habit of being in a wrong state. Though you were born with the ability to generate a vast range of different states, people develop a personal repertoire, and some of these become habitual. It's easy to get so used to these that you don't even notice them; you may even think they're part of your nature. You may be quite content to be thought of as 'cheerful' – but what if you are thought of as 'depressive', 'grumpy', 'pessimistic'? Recognising that these may simply be habitual states rather than an innate part of your personality can mean you feel more able to change. Perhaps you're not depressive after all. Maybe it's just a state you've got used to. Not exactly comfortable, and certainly not consciously chosen – just familiar.

Haste, anxiety and anger are all examples of states which can block your ability to enter into Inner Coaching. So, in a different way, can sadness, depression or indecision. Each tends to swallow you up, so that you're not able to engage with inner exploration, speculation, discussion or negotiation. You're simply not available.

Getting in the right state

So if you recognise that you're in the wrong state, whether infrequently or habitually, how can you get in the 'right' one – and how will you know?

Sometimes life seems to provide a 'wake-up call' – a major event or life change which simply forces you to think and to stop taking yourself for granted. Normal life transitions such as leaving home or university, getting married, becoming a parent or getting a qualification can make you rethink who you are, how you feel and what you want.

Often, such a state change can involve profound self-questioning. How can I be a parent and provide security and certainty for my children when I still feel uncertain about my own life? How can I manage others now that I've been promoted when I still feel like an ordinary worker myself? Who am I now that I've retired? It is entirely fitting that the words 'state' and 'status' both derive from the same Latin root. A change of status can cause a major change in state, and this can leave people questioning their identity and purpose in life.

Similar dislocations and rethinking can be caused by the onset of major illness or by bereavement. Again, the accepted status quo (that word again) has been disrupted. People who have been caught up in patterns of addiction, whether it's to drugs, alcohol or abusive relationships, may experience a similar 'moment of truth' at a particularly low point in their pattern. Dramatic events like these provide a pretty powerful negative impetus for getting into a better state, and they do so by breaking the state that currently exists. It literally can't go on.

INNER COACHING TIPS: CHANGING STATES

New knowledge, changed circumstances, changed feelings and changed physiology are the key to changing states. By deliberately changing any one of these elements, you can change an existing state at will.

▶ The simplest way to change state is to change your physiology. If you're sitting, stand and move. If you're hunched, straighten up. If you are feeling slow and lethargic, try running on the spot for a few moments. If you're rushing about, make yourself sit down for a few moments and take stock.

▶ Or you can change your posture, as Wendy did when at 17 she had an interview for a place at Oxford and was called in to see the college principal. As she began answering the principal's questions she became aware of how tense she felt, and noticed that she was sitting on the edge of the chair, all hunched over. *'I don't usually sit like this,'* she thought, and deliberately made herself sit back in a more relaxed posture. She changed her posture – and her state changed with it.

▶ If your thoughts are running away with you, and you realise you're creating a disaster scenario, simply think *'STOP!'* If it helps, say it out loud. If you are a film buff, shout *'CUT!'* Thump your fist on your knee or the arm of your chair – firmly, not painfully. What would you rather be thinking? Maybe you need to rescue the scenario and give it a better ending. Or maybe you need to think about something which makes you feel strong and capable so that you can return to your problem in a stronger frame of mind.

What's right for you

So how do you get in the right state for Inner Coaching? And just what is the right state for you?

There are many different kinds of right state, and the art is to find what helps *you*. You are aiming to be available to yourself, which means being free from external distractions or things that engage your logical processing much too much. You want to enter new territory, to discover what you don't yet know that you know. You are aiming to have what can truly be called an 'open mind', to be reflective and curious, to wonder and to notice, to trust that what you experience here and now in these moments is informative and of value even if it's not immediately understandable. You are aiming for that state of curiosity and exploration which is at the heart of coaching. These are the characteristics of the right state, and you're looking to identify anything that helps you nourish your ability to enter it.

One way is to follow the guidelines we've given to create a mindful state (page 10). But what if you don't have the time, or the space? Then you'll need to access one of your hidden resources: even if you don't realise it, you have inside you your own internal blueprint for just the kind of state you need. If you think about the last time you felt reflective and open to your own thoughts and feelings, it's likely to have occurred quite naturally and spontaneously, almost 'by accident'. What were you doing? Perhaps you were staring out of the window at work, sipping your first coffee of the day and waiting for a phone call. Maybe you were doing the ironing, or mowing the lawn. You might have been walking the dog – or just walking. You could have been jogging, swimming, knitting, tinkering with the car or gardening.

What do these activities have in common? They all occupy your attention, but peripherally. Many of them have a repetitive or rhythmical quality. They allow a bit of your mind to be free-floating. And so they allow you, quite naturally, to dip into that other part of yourself – the wisdom within. You may remember that elusive piece of information as you load up the washing machine. You may find the answer to that irritating little problem just arrives with you on the doorstep at the end of the walk. One friend was 'wool-gathering' as a colleague delivered a tedious presentation when a wonderful decorating scheme for her new house suddenly 'arrived' in her mind. In this kind of state, you may find your internal coach prompting you to ask that deeper question, find that more profound understanding, reach that larger solution.

Once you've found the right activity, you'll find a state that's just right for you. There are likely to be others, once you search for them. But you can access this state right now:

▶ You can engage in the same activity again as soon as possible.

▶ You can stare into space (or shut your eyes) for a moment and just remember how you felt – and notice how this changes your state even as you think about it.

INNER COACHING EXERCISE: NURTURING THE STATES THAT WORK FOR YOU

If you want to build the habit of internal exploration, build a habit of nurturing such naturally occurring states in your own life – and of cherishing the information that comes to you through them. The philosopher Sören Kirkegaard said, 'I walk myself into many of my best ideas,' and we both find that a 20-minute walk at the beginning of the day not only energises and loosens us up, but also promotes creative thinking.

▶ You could do this too. If you don't have the time at the beginning of your day, when do you have it? Maybe you have to walk to catch the bus to work, or to pick up the children from school, or to the shops ...? While it's easy to regard these chunks of time as 'fillers' between activities that 'really matter', it's equally easy to reclaim them for your Inner Coaching – something that will transform these daily routines into ways of enriching, invigorating and enhancing your life.

▶ What other everyday activities give you this free-floating feeling?

▶ Notice how you are breathing. The chances are that when you are in this state your breathing pattern is slower and shallower or more regular and deeper than at other times. Go with your breathing pattern.

▶ If you are doing something rhythmical, what kind of a rhythm is it? Experiment by making it slower and faster to find the rhythm that's exactly right for you. Without even knowing it, you're likely to have established your own comfortable pace. Is the same rhythm involved in other activities that create similar states for you? If so, the chances are that your brain-wave patterns are similar in each – in other words, you're in an alpha state.

What works for one person won't necessarily work for another. The trick is to find what works for you.

Giving yourself permission

It's a curious feature of Western society that many people find it more acceptable to 'switch off' through artificial means like alcohol than through natural ones – perhaps because natural switching off, however briefly, makes you less available to others. Have you ever gone off inside your head for a moment only to have someone wave their hand in front of your eyes in order to reclaim your attention? Perhaps you've done this to someone else. However friendly the context, what's happened is that the internal exploration has been spotted, and stopped. It really is as brutal as that.

You can do this to yourself, too. You can catch yourself out as you daydream, just as perhaps a parent or teacher did long ago. *'Pay attention!'* you think. You can make yourself feel guilty just as they did. And you can curtail your inner exploration in a flash.

We're inviting you to reconsider, to give yourself permission – even to positively encourage these shifts in focus, because they are the gateway to your inner wisdom. It's not selfish to take the opportunity; it's self-caring and self-enhancing.

Knowing when you're in this special state

All of us have daydreamed, so we have all experienced the right, receptive state for Inner Coaching. But we may not have fully realised it. Realising this is like learning to see: babies receive a huge amount of information through their eyes, yet they have to learn to distinguish *what* they're seeing. The rare people who have been born blind and have their sight restored in adult life often find this extremely difficult. And given that this special state of internal preoccupation is so often discouraged by others, it's all too easy to fail to stay in it long enough to find out what it's like and what it offers. You need to trust it – and yourself.

How will you recognise that you're in this special, receptive state? The litmus tests are kinaesthetic, just as they are for every other state. There will be differences in how your body is and how you feel physically and emotionally. Externally, you may become very still, even if it's only for a few moments, and your facial muscles will relax. Your face may lose expression. Your pupils will enlarge as you stop focusing on the outside world. It's likely you'll feel comfortable or relaxed, or at ease in yourself even if you're moving. You may feel almost suspended. Time may seem to stop. And happily, you can enter into this state quickly and deliberately, to use it for Inner Coaching.

Test it out, right now, and discover another way you can steer your Inner Coaching. Read through all the steps before you begin.

INNER COACHING EXERCISE: ENTERING THAT SPECIAL STATE

▶ Think of a question you'd really like to ask yourself: it might be about why you find it difficult to do something; it might be about how you'd make the best decision; it might be what you'd really like to achieve; it might be about the next step; it might be about what's really important for you to be mindful of right now.

▶ Put the book down, uncross your legs so that your legs support you in balance, and stare into space. Look through whatever it is you're staring at. Have 'soft eyes'.

▶ Notice what you notice. Adjust any muscles that are tight or uncomfortable so that they relax. Allow your breathing to deepen and settle.

▶ Allow the question or issue that you want to focus on to settle into your awareness. But whereas in a different state, you might 'think it over' or 'turn it around', 'argue it out' or 'have a good look at it', instead just allow it simply to be present. Is there a new way for you to understand it? How could you manage it better? What might you have overlooked, or failed to understand?

It's important to recognise that often the answers don't come immediately. Sometimes you'll even have a sense somewhere that you're 'processing ... processing ...' Monitor your state rather than the answers you may get. There will be responses, even just to bringing the issue to your own attention. And these will tell you whether it's sufficient simply to 'post it' and then reconnect with the everyday world again, or whether you need more time for reflection and inner communication. Your conscious mind can't give you the answers to these kinds of questions, because they're outside its scope.

States summed up

Let's just recap one of the simplest ways of all to put yourself into the right state to explore something important to you.

INNER COACHING EXERCISE: MAKING SPACE

▶ Let your eyes go out of focus. (Let them shut if you are seated and if it seems to happen naturally.)

▶ Become aware of your breathing and allow it to slow down naturally as you pay attention to it and allow your awareness to turn inwards.

▶ Have a sense of these moments giving you access to a wider range of your own resourcefulness, as seeds which can germinate at the right time into new insight or new strategies.

▶ Create a neutral and welcoming space in your awareness and allow the issue or question you want to ask yourself to enter it.

▶ Give yourself a little more time simply to enjoy being with yourself in this special state, or simply resume what you were doing.

Changing state is a skill you're born with, and you'll rapidly become familiar with it and even comfortable using it for Inner Coaching, wherever you are and whatever you're doing. As you build your habit of connecting with yourself internally, you'll begin to build information and evidence of how much more you know about yourself and your world than you may previously have thought. Things that were puzzling may suddenly become clearer. Feelings that were confusing may become understandable. Behaviours that limited you become explainable – and then you can use Inner Coaching to help you change them as you find better ways to achieve the same things. As you get into the habit of entering your Inner Coaching state, you may also start to find that the communication doesn't just have to be one-way. Sometimes ideas, suggestions and questions come to you 'from nowhere' – except you now know that they're from other dimensions of yourself. And this tells you that you're building trust into the relationship between you and yourself. With connectedness and trust, you can begin whole new voyages of discovery.

INNER COACHING TIPS: MASTERING STATES

▶ Notice your 'trough' moments.

▶ Cultivate your other naturally occurring mindful states.

▶ Look for recurring patterns: time, place, activities and triggers.

▶ Work with all these mindful states by 'posting' notice of your needs, issues and queries. Respect any responses you get as valid data, whether they reach you immediately or later, and whether or not they make logical sense.

▶ Change state deliberately, using the different methods we've outlined:

- when you are stressed

- when you are upset or angry

- when you are confused

- when you are in the grip of any strong emotion

And ask yourself how best you can use your inner resources to handle the situation.

Chapter Five

Avoiding Self-sabotage

I n the last chapter we showed you how you can recognise a state that favours Inner Coaching, and how you can use it to access your internal wisdom to tackle important questions. Sometimes these questions are about immediate decisions and needs. Sometimes they are about much bigger issues, like finding your direction in life. And of course, Inner Coaching gives you ways to relate the one to the other – to set the smaller goal in its context as part of the larger quest.

In the West, people are accustomed to valuing individual fulfilment very highly. However, we recognise that for people in some cultures, fitting in is more important than standing out. Whatever the balance, Inner Coaching will be valuable. Specifically, you can use it to help you find your own path in life and negotiate the tasks and roles that challenge you.

The things that deter you from your journey, or tempt you off-course, will be precisely those things which you are personally most likely to respond to. If your quest is for new experience, you may find difficulty in deciding which of the new experiences that life presents are truly promising for you, and which are going to turn out to be blind alleys. You may also be led astray by what you already know and can do just because it's familiar and attending to it seems natural and easy. Or perhaps, like a colleague of ours, you may enjoy having many talents but have trouble managing them. And you can also find yourself side-tracked by your own attitudes and ways of thinking.

In this chapter we're going to alert you to some important processes which can sabotage your personal quest. They are insidious precisely because they don't *seem* like enemies: in fact, they usually promise you real benefits. That's why they're so hard to resist. We're going to explore just how they are seductive, and how you can keep on track with your Inner Coaching and still find a way to have at least some of the benefits they promise, without paying the very high price they exact.

Song of the Sirens

We think of these diverting processes as similar to the Sirens, the creatures in Greek mythology who lured sailors toward their island by the seductiveness of their appearance and the sweetness of their singing. As the sailors altered their course and came closer, many were wrecked on the rocks surrounding their island. Those who succeeded in landing became the Sirens' slaves. This is the reason why Odysseus, on his voyage home, gave orders to his men to put wax in their ears to deafen them, and to lash him to the mast so that he would be unable to steer the ship towards their island and away from its true course.

Whatever your personal journey, there are five Sirens you need to beware of:

- Sabotage by your own internal dialogue

- Assuming negative intent

- Suspicious scepticism

- Cynicism

- Fantasising.

Each of these, in its own way, stops you getting into the open and available state you need for Inner Coaching and denies you access to the wisdom within you by offering you something that seems valuable. Like all seductions, these can be instant and immediate or incremental and insidious. The ultimate result is the same: you go off course. The five Sirens all promise more than they actually deliver. They cheat you. They set you against yourself.

The Sirens all offer false hope. Each can distract you from your path of personal exploration and self-realisation. They also tend to deny or undermine mystery – whether it's the mystery of Inner Coaching, self-exploration, faith in a personal quest, or honouring a value or belief.

By contrast, Inner Coaching won't make you feel cut off from yourself, and it will help you explore and clarify your personal path in life at many levels, from daily purposefulness to a life-long sense of identity and mission. And the paradox is that if you are truly willing to explore just how these Sirens may at times have a grip on you, you will through that very commitment to yourself be evading their clutches.

We've said that each of these Sirens can act to block your access to Inner Coaching. But there's an important paradox here. Asking yourself, for example, *'Just how and when am I suspiciously sceptical, and how is that different from when I'm rightly sceptical?'* is in itself an Inner Coaching question, whether or not you have chosen to enter that state first. You can't answer it in any way that feels meaningful to you except by connecting with yourself. The question, in other words, can actually help trigger the state you need to find the answer.

Siren 1. Sabotage by your own internal dialogue

Many people have got so used to their internal conversations that they barely register them, still less assess their effects; yet this internal dialogue can be extremely powerful. Let's look at what it involves, what's positive about it – and how, on the other hand, it can stop you from being available for Inner Coaching.

Most people, at one time or another, have carried on a kind of running internal commentary about what's happening. You can get into internal debates or even arguments with yourself about a decision or a choice. Sometimes you can encourage yourself – or give yourself a hard time about something. These internal conversations come naturally – and they can be very powerful simply because they're so familiar a way of thinking that you don't usually stop to examine the content or the tone in which it's being said. What positive things can this kind of self-talk achieve?

- It can give you the ability to talk things through with yourself. Where a complex calculation or issue is involved, this can help clarify it. Where you've a decision to make, it helps to separate out the differing points of view so that you can 'argue the case'.

- When you discuss something with yourself like this, hearing out the debate can allow you to consider 'your' own position.

- Sometimes what you're getting is a replay of something someone else said. This can be very helpful when you're unsure or lacking confidence. You might be reassuring yourself after an illness, for example, by reminding yourself that it takes time to build up strength again. This might be something you heard from your mother when you were little, or from your doctor at the surgery last week, or it might be folk wisdom – something 'everyone knows'. You've taken such information on board in the past, and now it's helpful to remind yourself of it.

- Another version of this process is when you have an intimate enough knowledge of how someone else would think or feel to be able to imagine even in their absence how they would respond to something. Your grandfather may have been dead for many years, but you can almost hear him warning you ... or encouraging you to go ahead ... You might even hear his familiar tone of voice and characteristic phrases, and incorporate it into your internal discussion.

So internal dialogue can be a helpful resource, and we will explore it further in Chapter 6. But like the Sirens, it can lead you astray or even wreck your Inner Coaching, which is our concern in this chapter. In itself, it's neither 'good' nor 'bad': that depends on the effects it has, and on how far you are able to take charge of its direction.

How do you distinguish between unhelpful internal dialogue and Inner Coaching? Well, Inner Coaching has a very different tone about it. It's not contentious or hectoring. It's not an argumentative debate. It also has rather different effects. You are likely to feel calm, curious, involved, surprised, stimulated, speculative ... You are likely to feel better about yourself. Even when some inner insight makes you realise you have been in error, you won't feel stupid or small. You will be focusing on what you need to do next, not on how bad you feel. Inner Coaching, unlike some internal dialogue, doesn't undermine your self-confidence.

Let's take some examples of this.

- Replaying critical comments to yourself. Often these come disguised in the form of helpful warnings, such as, *'Now don't go putting your foot in it.'* Because of the way this sentence is constructed, you cannot avoid focusing your attention on the very thing you're trying to avoid – putting your foot in it. There isn't anything else in that sentence to think of! And as you take the idea on board, you begin to imagine ways in which you might put your foot in it. This can have two effects: one is that you simply lose confidence and become hesitant or tongue-tied in the situation when it happens; the other is that you inexplicably find yourself doing the very thing you're dreading most – putting your foot in it. Your performance has been wrecked by the Siren of internal dialogue.

- Playing an outdated message. Something that made good sense when you were a child may not be so relevant when you're grown up.

- Acting on your internal dialogue without taking steps to verify that it has current value. It's easy to do this because internal dialogue is so familiar that it often takes place just outside the threshold of your conscious awareness. For example, you could 'talk yourself into' feeling or believing something, and react according to that without first checking the accuracy of your perception. Suppose that a friend who normally sends you a birthday card doesn't send you one this year. *'What have I done to offend him?'* you might say to yourself. Or, on the other hand, *'Perhaps I'm not grand enough for him now that he's become a doctor.'* You might even act on this, like someone we knew, who sent off a tetchy email of complaint, only to discover that his friend had been in hospital with a broken pelvis after a skiing accident. His internal dialogue had led him so far astray from any outer reality that it almost cost him the friendship.

Since internal dialogue can be both helpful and potentially destructive, you need to catch yourself at it and to become more aware of what kind you're engaging in. And it's not just the words that matter. Think about this sentence:

I wouldn't do that.

What happens if you play with different emphases?

I wouldn't do that = *Though other people might*

I *wouldn't* do that (sounds more threatening) = *Don't do it*

I wouldn't do *that* = *Do almost anything else.*

Emphasis alone creates different meanings. Then you can experiment to discover how tone also affects meaning. Try saying the same sentence to yourself in a caring way, in a threatening way, in an angry way, in a reassuring way. The thing to remember is that when you're talking, *you're also listening*. And as you listen, your state is being affected. Critical self-talk may make you feel small. Encouraging self-talk may give you courage. Reflective internal commentary can help you feel both more grounded and more protected when there's a practical or emotional emergency. Conflicting internal debate can exhaust you and make you feel fragmented. This kind of internal dialogue closes down your availability to your Inner Coaching because it rushes to judgement prematurely, doesn't notice what kind of assumptions it's founded on and ceases to be exploratory or reflective.

Pitfalls to be wary of include the following:

- Doing too much internal dialogue or relying too much on it – you need to become more connected to the external world.

- Doing too little – you need to encourage yourself to take time to become more self-reflective.

- Allowing the wrong kind of self-talk to continue unmonitored or unchecked – pause, reflect and if necessary amend!

INNER COACHING TIP: BECOME ALERT TO YOUR INTERNAL DIALOGUE

Once you are aware of the nature and the impact of your internal dialogue, you are in a position to alter it or to reinforce it.

First steps

▶ Become more attentive to your internal dialogue.

▶ Discover your personal patterns. When do you do it? when do you not do it?

▶ When would it be helpful to do more (such as, instead of simply reacting in a crisis or instantly acting out strong feelings)?

▶ Discover just who's involved your internal dialogue. It it spoken in someone else's external voice? Is it one bit of you haranguing another? Is it a debate between two or more parts of you?

▶ Who *isn't* involved in it that usefully could be?

▶ How useful is it to you?

▶ What's the tone?

▶ What impact is it having on your state?

▶ What effect does it have on your behaviour?

Answering these questions will give you lots of useful information. How are you going to use it to change the dialogue?

Next steps
This is how you can take charge of your internal dialogue:

▶ Change the words.

▶ Change the tone.

▶ Separate out other people's voices and views from your own. Remind yourself, for example, that that was someone else's maxim. It doesn't have to be yours. Invent a more appropriate one. Repeat the new one to yourself until it feels really familiar and authentic.

▶ Update the past. If it helps, write the story down, making sure you catch the wording as exactly as possible. Add *'That was then'* at the end. Write a new version of the story with today's updated understanding. Change the old message or punchline to one that's more relevant today. Write that down too. Someone we worked with wrote that when he was seven he was the last person to be picked for the team; he cried, and the class bully jeered at him for being 'feeble and wet'. 'Nobody wants a cry-baby on their team!' he said. Then he went on: 'But that was then. Now I know that I had many talents and grew up to use them well. Among them was a talent for compassion – and a talent for athletics.' And he added his own punchline. *'I enjoy both my strength and my tenderness – I enjoy being me.'*

Siren 2. Assuming negative intent

We can't function in life without making assumptions. And the assumptions you make about yourself, as we began to show in Chapter 2, can have great impact on your ability to approach yourself and access your hidden resources through Inner Coaching. In that chapter we listed some enabling assumptions you can make about yourself. Here we want to look at some which are potentially very destructive.

Assumptions derive from past experience and from lessons deliberately taught to us. They are the mental tramlines which can guide – or limit – our thinking, feeling and behaviour. A fundamental set of assumptions that we all carry concerns other people's attitudes towards us: do we think they're benevolent, or are they negative? And we can also make similar assumptions about ourselves – in particular, about those parts of our being that we're less knowledgeable about and about bits of ourselves that seem to drive emotions or behaviours we don't like.

In a way, making such assumptions is like being mildly paranoid. With this mindset it's as if you're looking around you to see what's wrong, who's after you, how you're being cheated or done out of your rights. You're assuming that this is how the world functions. When you don't understand something, in particular, you're inclined to think it's directed against you.

Is there any value in making such negative assumptions? Certainly, we learn from our experience, and one way we do this is by generalising from a specific incident, rather as a stain may spread outwards from an initial spot. If you were frightened by a dog when you were little, you may become suspicious not just of that dog but, by degrees, of all dogs; you're trying to protect yourself against being frightened again. *Once bitten, twice shy.* If you were cheated by a used-car salesman, you may be suspicious of others – and perhaps tend to prefer buying things at list price rather than second-hand in future.

We knew someone who had become very wary of redheaded people when she was about eight. She had a serious illness and was sent to live with relatives in the country – and quite coincidentally, her parents let the spare room to a redheaded lodger. She associated redheads with being sent away (which was what it felt like to her). Many years later her son started going out with a redhead. She told herself that she had to warn him that redheads couldn't be trusted, and it was only his incredulous and angry reaction that made her realise what was going on.

When you have a bad experience it makes sense to be on guard against it happening again. This is where assumptions come in. Negative judgements normally begin with a specific example, but in building a wider assumption that's intended to help you avoid trouble or pain in the future you start to generalise. And that means you don't examine the evidence. 'All men are bastards', a client says after a bad break-up. She's generalised: does she really mean 'men everywhere throughout all human history'? (Has she met them all?)

The second Siren can also operate internally, setting you against yourself. When you've let yourself down in the past, you may label it a 'self-destructive pattern' or 'a bad habit'. You assume this aspect of you is negative and can't be changed. You simply can't resist cream buns? You won't let yourself relax into intimacy in a relationship but are always a little on guard, a little removed? You think of yourself as weak-willed, or berate yourself for being aloof or frigid, selfish or whatever. Doubting yourself can be profoundly distressing – and tiring. You always have to be on the lookout lest you betray yourself or let yourself down.

These powerful yet apparently discordant impulses within you also have their point of view, and their rationale. Perhaps the distancing part of you is trying to protect you against hurt – or against becoming vulnerable through being too transparent in your relationship. Perhaps the bit of you that just loves cream buns is trying to ensure that you get some rewards, or some fun, or 'something sweet in life'.

Assuming negative intent, whether on the part of others or of yourself, can make you uneasy or unhappy. But it can also do more than this. It can lead you to behave in such a way that the thing you dread most actually comes about. When we look out for something, that's what we see – unconsciously, we're selecting for it. In very subtle ways, believing others are out to do you down tends to make sure you end up connecting with people who do just that.

An acquaintance of ours ran her own business, and was always complaining about the 'disloyalty' of people she encountered. She felt they agreed to deals and arrangements and then failed to keep their promises. Yet she often got involved with people who had problems with boundaries and agreements. Between them, they made informal, word-of-mouth arrangements which were fuzzy and which both parties tended to forget or remember differently. Not surprisingly, her business often ran into problems around contracts, reliability and boundaries.

If, on the other hand, you assume the majority of other people are well-intentioned, you are also likely to find events prove you right. That doesn't mean you need to be Pollyannaish. As the proverb says, *Trust in Allah – but first tie your camel*. It's the same if you assume that different – even very different – parts of yourself are well-intentioned. Or if you assume that life itself is. Some years ago Wendy and her family had a young horse that suddenly became ill and had to be destroyed. While they were waiting for the vet to arrive, someone at the yard, trying to be comforting, said to Wendy: 'Life's a bitch, isn't it.' Wendy remembers thinking – and replying – 'No!' Because she didn't make that assumption about life, this tragic happening, far from 'proving' such a negative belief, stood out as an exception in her experience.

INNER COACHING TIPS

▶ Find out what kind of assumptions you're making. This may be an uncomfortable process, but it's the first step towards assessing their validity and usefulness.

▶ Ask yourself where a particular assumption comes from. Is it the result of something that happened to you in the past? Did you simply take it on board from someone else? One of our clients had 'inherited' a maxim from his father: *Never volunteer.* For our client, it was important to recognise that this maxim may once have been valid for his father. But that doesn't mean it should hold true in all circumstances, and it might not be true for him at all.

▶ Test your generalisations. This is the key reality check. *All* men? *All* cream buns? Take a habit of your own that you mistrust and allow yourself to wonder what positive intent might possibly underlie it. Spell out what its results actually are. Do the cream buns contribute to your being overweight? Could being overweight possibly be advantageous to you in some way? Perhaps, like a client of Ian's, your sheer bulk may give you a feeling of gravitas, or substance. Or it may protect you, newly divorced, from the vulnerability of being a free agent again: you may tell yourself you should enjoy partying, but deep down you're frightened of being hurt again. It's easier to cushion yourself in a layer of fat which you think you don't want.

Siren 3. Suspicious scepticism

The lure of suspicious scepticism is that it offers to protect you against being let down. And that's a pretty powerful incentive – *'Won't get fooled again.'* The benefit you seem to get from being suspicious is that you're not easily taken in. You maintain a watchfulness. You look before you leap. When someone offers you something, you wonder, *'What's the catch?'* Where there really is a catch, of course, you're well prepared. But what if there isn't? Seeking certainty means you're perpetually wanting more evidence – and rather expecting that it will be negative. If it is, you won't be caught out. But with this attitude you'll find it difficult to trust and enjoy even when the gift, or the experience, or the person, seems to be genuine. The signature phrase of such suspicious scepticism, *It ain't necessarily so,* works both ways. And it limits your ability to get involved in Inner Coaching, because it constantly intrudes with its undermining attitude. It can undermine your trust in the benefits of the process or of your ability to engage in it. Both of these damage the openness, enquiry and self-trust you are seeking to develop. Being suspicious tends to mean that you stay on the fence. You're always somewhat distant, and always waiting.

Why is such suspicious scepticism one of the Sirens that threaten your inner exploration and your personal quest for meaning and fulfilment? Because it makes you mistrustful: of others, of experience, even of yourself. It stops you committing – to anything. It is likely to make you doubtful about anything whose workings are not fully apparent. You just can't be sure if your instinct is trustworthy, if your enjoyment is wholehearted, if it's right to get involved. This kind of suspicious scepticism is a play-safe mechanism, and it is largely reactive to external events rather than proactive about them. It doesn't like you to launch into the unknown.

So you may find yourself being doubtful about anything that promises good experiences or good results. *'Really?'* you say to yourself as you read. *'Can anything be that good?'* Or you try something out, and are then suspicious of the results you get. *'Maybe that was just luck,'* you think. *'Perhaps it would have happened anyway.'* There are no cast-iron comebacks to your specific doubts about you; but there is plenty of evidence that thousands of other people have learnt and benefited from this process.

People who have visited the remote places of the world often use words like 'awesome'. They also bring back a fuller sense of what it means to live on this planet, and often a deeper sense of their own humanity. We'd like you to give yourself permission to explore your own remote places and, like those travellers, discover how awesome and enriching this can be. And for that to happen, you need to set suspicion aside. It's not the protective mechanism it seems to be, because it already presumes the worst. It's a loaded judgement disguising itself as an attitude of rational enquiry.

So how can you retain the benefits of rational scepticism without becoming suspicious and loading the odds? In our experience you don't have to make a choice between leaping right into something or hanging back. Though being suspicious may protect you against some risks, it can equally cut you off from the joys of full involvement.

When you commit yourself to yourself through Inner Coaching, you need to accept that there can never be complete evidence for or against anything, and be willing to trust your intuition rather than waiting for the certainty that can never be. It's about developing trust, ultimately, in yourself.

In Shakespeare's *The Merchant of Venice*, the hero Bassanio has to make a choice between three caskets – gold, silver and lead – if he is to attain the woman he loves. The gold one promises the chooser 'what men may desire'; the silver, 'as much as he deserves'. The leaden casket carries the legend: 'Who chooses me must give and hazard all he hath'. The heroine Portia's first suitor rejects risk and chooses gold. Yet Bassanio, less sceptical and more aware of what love really entails, chooses lead – and gains the lady he loves.

INNER COACHING TIPS

▶ Use a healthy scepticism as a first-line defence, evaluating events, possibilities and people and rejecting those which are likely to do you harm. It is at this point that you need to allow yourself to make a leap, relying on that other wisdom – the wisdom within – to guide you in evaluating what has passed that first test.

▶ Be cautious with people or circumstances you don't yet know, that are exaggerated or overblown, and with things which are manifestly to someone else's advantage, rather than suspicious of them.

Caution can offer you an initial way of filtering what's valuable and trustworthy from what's not.

▶ Look for evidence, and be prepared to update and refine your judgements as more comes in.

▶ Run a check on people or situations that have let you down in the past. Might they be influencing your present judgement inappropriately?

▶ Now it makes sense to embark on a less hard and fast kind of exploration. Through your Inner Coaching, consult your inner wisdom. What do your gut feelings tell you about this person, this opportunity, this amazing offer?

Used like this as a first filter, scepticism can be a useful warning beacon or channel marker that helps guide you on your way, rather than the Siren of suspicion preventing you from taking the next step on your path.

Siren 4. Cynicism

Cynicism goes one stage further towards disbelief than suspicious scepticism, and it's a harder state to get out of. In fact, it can block you from trying out anything different or new. When you recognise it in yourself or others, we suggest you think of it as a sign of extreme disappointment and an attempt to protect yourself against being wounded again. It's an attitude of *Get them before they get you.* If you have no hope and no faith, the contorted logic goes, you'll never be disappointed. Cynicism blocks trust, exploration, speculation and openness to new experiences and new ideas. It could prevent you from getting into Inner Coaching at all, or put a full stop to it at any point in the process, because it blocks your availability to yourself.

You need to begin by accepting that cynicism, like any other habit, is rooted in a desire to look after yourself. And then you need to find out more. You can do this at any point when you recognise that downputting *'Oh yeah?'* feeling in yourself.

If you are being cynical, what kinds of things are you being cynical about? Some you may have in common with other people. Your target may be politicians, for example, or certain kinds of salesmen. But maybe it's your spouse. People, experiences, theories, systems and governments can all let you down. So they are common targets of people's cynicism. On the other hand, few people are cynical about their pets. One reason why this might be is that pets accept us without reservation or criticism. It's hard to be cynical about that kind of affection – nor do we need to be, because it doesn't let us down.

In adopting cynicism as a defence, you may actually be making a poor deal, for you have to give up many things which could make your life a delight: hope, trust, excitement, daring, faith, involvement. It's a high price to pay for protection – and one which betrays its own promise of security by wrecking you on the bitter rocks of disillusion, doubt and remoteness. You're never at the party, only peering disdainfully through the window. And like that outsider, you may get to have a sneaking feeling that you're really missing out. You are.

Cynicism promises immunity from further disappointment or pain: that's its seductive pull. Yet you have within your repertoire better ways of protecting yourself, if you use them judiciously.

INNER COACHING TIPS

▶ Track your cynicism back so that you find out what it's trying to protect you from. It's likely to involve fearing being let down or taken in some way.

▶ When you encounter something or someone new, pay attention to your immediate response. If you're immediately cynical, check why, and ask yourself, 'Is this justified?'

▶ Take time to identify what you are *not* cynical about. Being able to trust in something is a basis you can build from. Perhaps for you it is a pet. Or a certain friend. Or yourself. Or a system of values and beliefs. Explore what it is about this that gives you confidence.

▶ Like suspicious scepticism, cynicism is a process that tends to spread and become more inclusive. Keep this in check by asking yourself, for example, if *all* politicians are truly fakes – at *all* times. Break down the generalisation until you find the specific examples which have really got through your defences.

> ▶ Have the courage to examine any wounding experiences that gave rise to your cynicism in the first place. Cynicism can be rather like a sticking plaster – it conceals the wound but doesn't actually heal it.

Siren 5. Fantasising

The great charm of the Sirens was that they offered a life of ease and pleasure. And fantasising offers the immediate pleasure of having the experiences you want, when you want them – in your own mind. The lure of escape via the spectator sport of fantasising about what might be is very different from Inner Coaching, which actually engages you actively and profoundly in moving towards getting it. And whereas fantasising never truly delivers in reality, Inner Coaching does. It's grounded in real situations, real feelings, real desires and real resources at many levels of your being, and helps you shape and create the reality of your experience both internally and externally.

Fantasising can seem very real when you're caught up in it – whether it's for moments or for years. Like Odysseus, who was lured by the enchantress Circe to spend years on her island instead of completing his quest, or the sailors led astray by the Sirens, you're caught up in what might be, in what you'd like to be, rather than in what actually is. Like them, you may be wanting to avoid 'hard reality'. Even if your life is pleasant, it's easy enough to get drawn into fantasy: many magazines play on this with lifestyle articles and offers. Advertising offers the promise of greater happiness and better looks if only we buy this or that product. And there's another kind of fantasising, too – the kind that gets you really gripped into imagining the kind of future you'd like but without actually doing anything towards making it come true.

In itself, fantasising is neither good nor bad – it is the foundation of many dreams that are brought alive through inspiration and hard work. It becomes a Siren in our sense when it's a substitute for action, or when it's not grounded in reality – actual or potential. It becomes a Siren when saccharine scenarios become a substitute for the genuine speculation and creativity that your Inner Coaching can foster.

There is another kind of fantasising, too, which arises from artificial state change. When you allow drugs or alcohol or tobacco or sex or power to encapsulate you in their artificially created pleasures, or when you mesmerise yourself through overly repetitive 'mindless' activities that absorb you in the short term, such as unselective television viewing or repeated games of computer solitaire, you enter into an artificially induced state that makes you sacrifice something genuine about yourself and your unique life purpose.

All these pleasurable seductions end with a bump. The highs they give are phoney. You pay the price of a hangover, of withdrawal symptoms, of knowing that hours, months or even years have gone by and you're no further forward. There's usually a sense of waste and disappointment. One way out is to go back for more – change the state again. You are becoming addicted. Genuine imaginings are grounded in real possibilities, and can be translated into real actions.

Less obvious perhaps than these is the seduction of comfort, where you never stretch or tax yourself or take risks. We all need comfort and security – but built into us also is the need for challenge and growth. Challenge and growth involve going beyond the known. Choosing to remain within your comfort zone in life means you are choosing not to grow, not to discover, not to enlarge or surprise yourself.

The Sirens of seductive pleasure and of comfort above all else are both culs-de-sac. In order to experience them, you must give up other things which are important and valuable: your time, your purpose, your potential, even your identity. Genuine pleasures don't end this way. They don't have to be repeated in ever higher and higher doses; they don't diminish who you are; they don't pull you off-course and leave you with regrets or a sense of shame; they don't cut you off from yourself, or isolate you from others or from the real world.

INNER COACHING TIPS

Ask yourself these questions. They will help you tell genuine pleasures and comforts from false ones:

▶ Do you feel regret afterwards?

▶ Are you missing out on other possibilities?

▶ Do you need to repeat, to do more, to up the dose?

▶ Do you feel a sense of waste?

▶ Do you have a sense of being cut off, or of withdrawal?

> ▶ Do you feel out of control?
>
> ▶ Do you ever feel the pleasure wasn't worth the price you paid for it?

If you have any of these feelings, there's a good chance that you've been seduced. By and large, choices that are in harmony with who you are and with your inner wisdom will feel deliberate, life-enhancing, worth the risk and worth what you've had to pay or forgo. You may make mistakes, or decide to change course, but you are more likely to feel that all you've learnt from the experience was that that it was a waste of time.

Confronting the Sirens with Inner Coaching

During this chapter we've given you a number of suggestions for testing out whether you're being seduced by any of these Sirens, and for discovering exactly what they're trying to protect you against. You may have deliberately used a mindful state to help you consider these issues. Even if you didn't, if you were really committed to the exploration we suggested, it's likely that you found yourself becoming more inwardly focused. As we said at the beginning, the questions and suggestions themselves are likely to have triggered an Inner Coaching state. And one of the intriguing powers of Inner Coaching, which we'll explore again later, is that you can use it to explore itself. You can use it to find out more about when and why it works, when and how it 'doesn't work' – provided you give yourself permission to ask.

It's our experience that when people are willing to search for answers within themselves, they can find the inner wisdom – the means to set themselves, and keep themselves, on course with their lives. And they also find the talismans and strengths that will keep them safe from the Sirens they may encounter on the way.

INNER COACHING EXERCISE: BEYOND THE SIRENS

> ▶ What Sirens are you most tempted by? What Sirens are most likely to lead you astray unawares?

▶ Quests are of many kinds. Some are aimed at remedying ills, some at enhancing the quality of life, some at achieving specific goals. Another kind of quest takes delight in exploring for its own sake. What kind of quest are you on?

▶ Use your Inner Coaching time whenever needed to consider just where and by how much you may be off course, and what will help you get back on track.

Chapter Six

Facing Your Fears

Fear is a normal part of being human, and it serves to warn and protect us. In this chapter we're going to look at the personal demons each of us fears, not as enemies to vanquish, but rather as inevitable parts of life which need to be *managed*, and which *can* be managed, with the help of the wisdom you have within you.

What place does fear have in a book on Inner Coaching? Fear can block your availability to Inner Coaching, because it generates – sometimes in an instant – intense state changes. In that moment when you're shaking with anxiety or paralysed with alarm, it can feel impossible to reflect, or explore inwardly. Yet when you face what you fear and use Inner Coaching to help you explore what it means and why it affects you, your fear can actually become a valuable resource.

Sounds contradictory? Yes. But we've found over the years that if people are willing to tolerate ambiguity and paradox and actively explore them, they often lead to important insights and valuable resources.

When you learn to take a contradiction as a signal to explore further, your Inner Coaching becomes so much richer and so much more productive. As a great scientist once said, the most exciting exclamation in science is not 'Eureka!' but 'That's odd ...' And although at first you may find it easier to do this internal exploration when you're in a calmer state, as you get used to Inner Coaching and become more able to do it instantly, anywhere, you'll learn to take even the very first signs of fearfulness as a signal to begin investigating.

Our personal demons

Each of us has our own personal demons, which are intimately related to our history and our particular vulnerabilities. If the Sirens seek to divert us through the power of their attractions, our personal demons can drive us away from our own resourcefulness and sense of purpose through fear. They can pursue us from the past, ensnare us in the present or lie in wait for us in the future. They have the power to wake us in the night, derail our normal thought processes, make us feel sick or scared, prevent us from doing things we want to do make us or compulsively do the things we don't want to. They block our openness and availability to our inner resources. Trauma, anxiety, panic attacks, rage, shame, fear can each involve the creation or remobilisation of such demons. Because these strong mind-body states temporarily take over our consciousness we can feel trapped and out of control.

In this chapter we're going to outline some ways in which you can begin to destabilise the hold of such demons on you and, better still, learn and grow through what your personal demons have to offer. Key to all this is the process of Inner Coaching, and it can be surprising and, in a strange way, heartening to discover that your demons can have a role here too. For ultimately, whatever circumstances originally brought a demon into being, once you learn to accept that you actually contribute to prolonging its existence you regain some choices. Through learning to understand the message the demon was trying to give you, rather than just trying to avoid it or run away from it, you regain some influence over your self and your situation and can begin to find new ways forward.

Demons are real because they really involve you. They catch you up in powerful experiences, powerful feelings and powerful reactions. Because you have the ability to recall, you can replay past events drawing on a full range of sensory experience: you can, in effect, have a terrifying experience all over again. Because you can imagine, you can also do all of this in advance of an event – whether or not things really turn out that way. So you can replicate bad times and have them twice, or imagine future ones without them ever happening in real life.

Your particular demons also affect what and how you learn. You can't *not* learn from what happens to you. The power of alarm, terror, sadness or grief shapes how you anticipate future experience. You learn to expect certain things, and you are also likely to evolve certain strategies for avoidance or for coping.

Imagining, and learning from experience, are both part of life. But you don't have to be the victim of either when you know how to transform their potentially negative impact or consequences through Inner Coaching.

How do your demons take away your power?

- They destroy your focus. When you're feeling strong feelings, you can't give what you're doing your full attention. If you're making a presentation at work, you may be worrying about whether you're making sense or sounding confused, about whether you're going to dry up – in your mouth or by running out of words. You may be trembling, shivering or blushing. You can't concentrate as you should – and then you also worry about how your colleagues are going to judge this dreadful performance. And that adds to your worries, and your confusion, and your lack of focus.

- Demons divide you against yourself, either because you're busy telling yourself off for being so stupid, weak or infantile, or because you simply can't be truly yourself.

- Demons weaken your confidence and lessen your ability to act. If you are running anxiety scenarios, or remembering past disasters, your confidence is going to be undermined. The word 'confidence' actually means 'faith in someone or something': you are in danger of losing much of your faith in ... *you*.

- Demons throw you off balance. This book is all about developing your access to the wisdom within you through the experience of Inner Coaching. But when you feel fearful or overwhelmed, you get alienated from your own wisdom. You stop being grounded, so you become even more vulnerable and more liable to be pushed this way and that. You may develop paranoid views, or your own fantasies may run away with you. You no longer know what to believe.

Whether they are real or imagined, past, present or future, internal or external, your demons can really get to you. In that sense, all demons are real, because they have real effects. Your reaction when you encounter an external demon, remember a past one or imagine one that might assail you in the future will be both lightning-fast and extreme. Fear is at the core of it – sometimes fear of the thing, sometimes fear of the fear itself. And when you feel fear you can feel powerless. Your personal power is sucked away and relocated in the thing you fear and your personal quest is interrupted.

Often, though, people are terrified not of creatures or things but of experiences: interviews, driving tests, speaking in public. Their terror may be related to past 'failures', or exist even when they know they always perform well in the event. And as we all know, you can also be afraid of being afraid. The danger then is that you start to make your world smaller and smaller as you try to avoid ever being upset. Don't do this, don't do that, just in case you meet a feared object, or a feared situation. You are actively giving away your own power.

Personal power

Power is all about ownership, and about choice. The word power comes from the same Latin source as the word 'potential' – a root word which means 'to be able'. Demons all affect your ability in one way or another. They make you less able – or actually *un*able – in a number of crucial spheres, affecting you in important ways.

1. Your freedom to act

If you are running scared, remembering or anticipating disasters, you'll hold back from action. You won't apply for that job, tackle a friend, boss, parent or partner about what's bugging you, or sign up to learn a new skill. Your demon will ensure that you try to keep within your known safety limits. Your freedom will be curtailed. You may spend time fantasising about what you'd really like to aim for in life, but resign yourself to doing without it, or putting up with second best.

2. Your ability to influence

Influence is the intentional and purposeful use of your power. It's directing your energy to bring about what you want. And it's a crucial component in owning yourself and shaping your own life. Who or what might you want to influence?

- First and foremost, yourself. Many people feel out of control, because they are unable to do what they want or do things they don't want to do, have feelings they'd prefer not to have, and feel at the mercy even of their own thought processes. *'I just can't seem to stop being this way ...'* Regaining power over your personal demons gives you back *yourself*. It doesn't mean, of course, that you will always be 'in control', because inevitably there will be times in your life when you will feel, think and do things you'd rather not – just because you're human. What it does mean is that you can cultivate your ability to observe yourself, catch yourself when you're straying off course, and have ways of bringing yourself back. Some of these we've already begun to explore, others you'll encounter as the book goes on. Influencing yourself also means that you have ways of working with your past, so that even though you can't change actual events, you can change your relationship to them, or the impact they will have from now on.

- Other people. Sometimes we feel that it's others who were, or are, the demons. And indeed we may have been hurt or victimised by them. One of the key steps in dealing with this particular demon, however, is to recognise the patterns that have resulted, and take ownership of your own part in continuing to replay them. This is a tough one, but it's vital if you want to stop continuing to empower those ancient demons in future.

- The situation. Influence works through individuals to affect situations. Owning your own power is about being able to shape what's going on now and what will happen in the future. Demons diminish your ability to do this too.

3. Your freedom to be wholly yourself without internal conflict

When you lack integrity and personal congruence it means that you feel divided within and from yourself. If your demon is disapproval, or the fear of failure, or the risk of being opposed to others, it can mean that you stop being authentic. You tolerate the intolerable. You don't defend yourself. You don't take risks. You don't realise your hidden potential.

Important parts of you are under wraps. You are no longer wholly the you that you could be.

INNER COACHING TIPS: HOW WE CREATE OUR OWN DEMONS

Life can create external demons for us, in the shape of traumatic experiences and their legacy of fear. But we can also manufacture our own. How? Check if you do any of these things:

▶ Split off parts of yourself – because you disapprove of them or because they are too painful to connect with. Bad habits, childhood traumas or, 'unworthy' thoughts can be targets for this process.

▶ Deny yourself. You may do this by habitually putting others first, or by simply not allowing yourself to have pleasurable experiences, whether they are everyday treats, major delights or ongoing rewards such as praise or the delights of the body.

▶ Suppress your own knowledge, feelings or wishes – things that you really know somewhere inside. You may ignore the messages that come to you from within, denying the validity of your dreams, giving yourself a hard time when you daydream, ignoring your body's aches and pains and warning signals. You may bombard yourself with oughts, musts and shoulds in an effort to bring yourself into line – with what?

▶ Engage in infighting. When you don't have open access to all parts of yourself, it's difficult to develop a way of working with conflicts between them. So you become the victim of internecine warfare – arguments that go on and on and round and round, with no winners, only losers. And the overall loser is you.

▶ Close down. It's not surprising that too much pain, too much confusion, too much conflict, too much self-denigration, can result in exhaustion. And when you're exhausted, you shut down. People can shut down on emotion, on their bodies, on their thoughts, on their wishes. To start with, it can feel quite restful – like stopping banging your head on the wall. But the *absence* of something isn't necessarily the *presence* of something else – when you shut down you create a void and become less alive, perhaps just a little, perhaps a lot. We remember a client who had used this strategy. In fact, he was aware of the process, and frightened by how it was spreading. When he first came for help he said: 'I've shut down on my feelings, I've shut down on my visions, I've shut down on hearing myself. If I shut down any more I shall die.' And he meant it. Working with him revealed how this strategy had begun as a way of handling a childhood trauma. Like all strategies, it had made sense at the time. But creating it meant that he had demonised all sensation and all emotion: they had to be avoided, so they got more frightening and the threat they represented got even greater. It snowballed. The external demon of hurtful experience had become an internal demon of self-manipulation. Our client knew that he was seeking help just in time.

However, once you have learned to re-engage with yourself through the process of Inner Coaching, setbacks, whether trivial or major, can become immediate signals that tell you it's time to connect with yourself. Becoming aware that you're off-course – in terms of feelings or goals – becomes a signal to use your personal Inner Coaching compass to find your direction again.

Turning your fear around

Finding the wisdom in your demons

When we revisit the dark places of our past we reclaim the power we left there.

This succinct summary of personal healing was written by one of our students many years ago. The process couldn't be better put. Your demons – terror, anxiety, anger, self-hatred and their ilk – represent a huge investment of your emotional energy. However they came into being, they have you tied up. We know from personal experience and from working with others that this can change.

Here's a six-step process you can use to learn from your fears and to begin to manage them effectively.

Step 1. Acknowledge what's actually happening

People who are good in emergencies tend to have a strategy to prevent becoming overwhelmed: they don't get into the feelings, they don't run future scenarios, they just focus on doing what's needed. Yet in other circumstances they may have plenty of feeling and lots of imagination. How do they do it?

They don't pretend the situation is anything other than how it is: they don't seek to minimise it or rationalise it away, and they don't allow themselves to dramatise or exaggerate it either.

Step 2. Change state

Use some of the skills you learnt in Chapter 4 to become aware of your state and find ways to change it. If you are panicky, rushed or in the grip of strong emotion, remind yourself that you cannot afford *not* to do something about it. Use the adrenaline to take a moment for yourself and *really notice just how strongly you're feeling.* That's how much you need your Inner Coaching right now!

Tuning in like this is actually a way to begin changing your state, for the very intentness of concentration you pay to the unpleasant feelings activates an inner focus – and begins to change your brain-wave patterns.

INNER COACHING EXERCISE: WAYS TO BEGIN CHANGING YOUR STATE

There is more you can do to change your state:

▶ You could clench your fist and really notice all the muscle tension there. As you relax it, become aware of how this affects your forearm, and the rest of your arm.

▶ Raise your shoulders high, hold them for a moment, then let them lower, breathing out as you do so. Notice how this begins to ease tension elsewhere in your body.

▶ Take a few breaths that are deep enough to raise your ribcage, letting each one out as slowly as you can. You'll find this makes it easier to take an even deeper one the next time.

> ▶ Imagine you are an outside helper in your own situation. You are concerned but not emotionally involved. How does the situation seem to you? Taxing? dangerous? alarming? uncertain? threatening but not life-threatening? Even when it's potentially a life-or-death situation, as in the case of a serious accident or illness, the helpful outsider is usually aiming to identify the immediate priorities. You can do that too – even if the person whose drama you are observing is you. This is a creative and useful way of harnessing the power inherent in the situation, because the adrenaline you generated through your alarm can now give you the energy you need for effective thinking and appropriate action.

Step 3. Seek out the demon's signal value

Earlier in the book we asked you to think about particular myths or stories you feel drawn to, and to consider what special meaning they have for you. You can do the same with demons. Why does a particular fear keep recurring in your life? Why this one?

A friend of ours had an intermittent fear of getting tetanus. His hobbies were extreme outdoor ones, and of course he was often getting scraped or cut, so there was usually some potential for infection. Yet it was only at certain times in his life that he found himself obsessing about whether he might have contracted tetanus. He knew it was a 'stupid' and obsessive fear, but somehow he couldn't stop. By using his Inner Coaching to consider the situation as a concerned observer, he realised that he had two questions to answer: one, why did this fear surface at these particular times and not others; and, two, how had his imagination made tetanus itself into a demon?

When he looked for the pattern linking the times when he felt afraid, he realised that on each occasion he had been worried about being stuck – in work or in a relationship. He had felt immobilised. Through Inner Coaching he realised that his inner wisdom had unconsciously seized upon tetanus as a symbol for what was happening because it was trying to alert him to what was going on. The terror had a purpose – it was meant as a wake-up call.

But why tetanus? The danger of being immobilised could just as well have been expressed by recurrent dreams of handcuffs, or leg-irons, or quicksand, or prison cells. Even though he was now aware of the terror's personal message, he continued to wonder about its origin. And one day the answer came. When he was little he fell off his bike, suffering severe cuts and concussion. His parents took him to casualty, where he was given a tetanus injection. In those days live serum was used, and he remembered overhearing the nurse warning his parents that as he tended to be allergic he should avoid having another tetanus shot in the near future – in case the combined dose caused him to develop the disease itself.

Remembering how the demon had first come into being, and recognising its signal value, meant that our friend no longer got caught up in this alarming fantasy. It also meant that he became more sensitive to hitherto unrecognised messages from within about how his life was going, so that when necessary he was able to make small adjustments in a calm spirit rather than needing a truly terrifying wake-up call to alert him to the perils of his own situation.

Step 4. Touch base with reality

Demons thrive on exaggeration. So it can be really helpful to cut them down to size. One way to do this is to use the very imagination that fuels them to disestablish their power.

INNER COACHING EXERCISE: SHRINKING YOUR DEMONS

▶ Run a worst-case scenario:

You're going to make a mess of that interview. You just know it.

What's the worst that can happen?

The manager will think you are a fool.

What's the worst that can happen?

Well, I won't get the promotion.

What's the worst that can happen?

I'll stay doing this job, fretting about the poor pay.

What's the worst that can happen?

> I might get so demotivated that my work suffers and I get the sack.
>
> *And the worst that will happen?*
>
> I might be unemployed, use up all my savings and lose my house.
>
> ▶ Now it's probably time to ask yourself the next reality-based question:
>
> *How likely is that?*
>
> Not very!

Usually, blowing your fears up into a grander and larger scale like this is sufficient in itself to explode the demon: there comes a point when like an overfilled balloon it bursts because it simply can't contain any more. But *should* there be a real danger hidden amongst the fantasy fears, the process will help you sift it out, and you will now know what it is.

Step 5. Deal with the specifics

Whether the inherent core of your demon is a past trauma, a present danger or a future fear, acknowledging it and identifying it from a position of concerned neutrality will allow you to work out what you need to do about it. In some cases, you may decide to seek the help of a therapist, coach or trainer. The key question for you to ask yourself at this stage in the process is:

'*So what now?*'

Yes, there is a difficulty – what *action* are you going to take? As soon as you take responsibility for your demon in this way, you reclaim the power you had invested in it.

Step 6. Get grounded again

Whether your particular demon is fear or one of the other destabilising emotions such as anger, regret, hatred, envy or jealousy, the process is the same. And the aim in each case is to re-establish your groundedness, both with yourself and with external circumstances. Only then can you regain your personal power and choose an appropriate and effective course of action.

INNER COACHING TIPS: SEEKING GROUNDEDNESS

Here are three ways to do this:

▶ Find ways to be at ease with past experiences that cannot be changed, such as those that caused you to feel anger, blame, shame or regret. The demons of the past can hold you prisoner in the present and prevent you from moving freely into the future. Yet the emotions generated by past events need to be respected, just because they were meaningful responses at the time. Plenty of people hold onto anger about past events, blame themselves or others for past inadequacies, or feel regret or shame for not having acted differently. '*I can't change the fact that I/he/they were wrong,*' they think. Indeed, past events cannot be changed – but our feelings about them and the meaning we make of them *can*. The threefold process of recognition, acknowledgement and taking action works here, too, as the following example shows.

Joanna had a dreadful argument with her sisters after their mother died. They wanted her, as a childless divorcee, to give their elderly father a home. But Joanna said no because she enjoyed her job and it took her abroad a great deal. She suggested that he sell the family home and buy a centrally located retirement flat with warden support. A major family row ensued. For a couple of years they saw practically nothing of each other, then the father had a heart attack and died. Joanna bitterly regretted both the estrangement and the fact that her father had died with the coldness between them unrepaired, but she knew it was harmful to keep on going over and over the events and wishing someone had acted differently.

She used her Inner Coaching to ask herself: '*What do I really want now?*' The answer was: '*I want to be talking with my sisters again, and seeing them now and again. I want the way to be open for us to see whether we can build a relationship again.*' And the solution that came to her was to write to them, tell them how she knew they all really loved each other and how much she wished they could find a way to mend things. She couldn't make them willing to forgive, but she could show that she was.

Whether you are struggling with regret like Joanna, or trying to cope with other powerful feelings about past mistakes or things you feel ashamed of, you can use your Inner Coaching to explore and acknowledge the issues involved, and then find the best way forward.

▶ Strengthen your base. It's one of the paradoxes in dealing with demons that the more you address them, the less power they have to damage or even frighten you. Whether your demons are people outside you or impulses, thoughts and patterns of your own, whether they're past traumas or future fears, the more you work with them, the more your potency increases. And as the Hobbit Frodo found with the tormented creature Gollum in Tolkien's *The Lord of the Rings*, an important first step is to assume that no one and no situation is entirely, absolutely, unreservedly bad.

This doesn't mean that we have to compromise our beliefs or our standards. We don't have to like others or forgive their actions, but we may come to understand what's going on. And that can restore our sense of personal worth and groundedness. It also creates a very different power relationship with them.

▶ Rebuild your integrity. What you're doing is rebuilding your sense of wholeness and personal honour. When you 'face the fear and do it anyway', you are allowing yourself to experience things which are very different – but without making yourself choose between them. When you make compromises from this personally grounded base, any concessions you make are deliberate and voluntary instead of accidental or unwilling and under the influence of others' agendas.

The Johari Window

In this chapter we have been exploring how your demons came to have power over you and what you can now do to reclaim that power. An underlying message is that getting to know yourself better is a powerful way to develop and to nurture the wisdom within.

The Johari Window gives us a useful description of the different dimensions involved. According to this model, there are four kinds of information about the self: (1) that which is unknown to yourself and unknown to others; (2) that which is known to yourself and unknown to others; (3) that which is known to others and unknown to you; and (4) that which is known to both you and others.

Johari Window

	Unknown to self	Known to self
Unknown to other	1	2
Known to other	3	4

When you use Inner Coaching to tune into a range of information from yourself that you were previously unaware of, you are moving items from Box 1 to Box 2. In becoming more aware of feedback from others about how they experience you, you are gaining access to Box 3. And as you choose to disclose information to others, you are opening up Box 4.

Demons are usually locked in Boxes 1 or 2. As you encounter them and actively seek to manage them, you allow them to move into more open spheres – and that in itself reduces their power, because the need to keep something secret in itself renders it even more powerful. A secret demon is even more terrifying than a known and open one. (If you're familiar with J.K. Rowling's Harry Potter, remember 'he who must not be named'?) This principle of owning and disclosing underpins the many 12-step programmes which have been derived from the original Alcoholics Anonymous model.

Once you have acknowledged your demons and learnt what they have to tell you, you are empowered in a different way – for the wholeness that comes with knowledge, self-acceptance and self-management is the greatest power of all. And Inner Coaching offers you a natural, powerful and ongoing means for doing all of this.

In Ursula Le Guin's mythical story *A Wizard of Earthsea,* the young hero, Ged, misuses his power as an apprentice magician and is pursued by a demonic being he has inadvertently called into the world. Its power grows as he grows in age and magical skill; for years he flees it, and then eventually he realises that he must turn and hunt it down. In that moment of insight he realises that the bond between them is his responsibility – and his choice.

It was a chase no longer. He was neither hunted nor hunter, now . . . He knew now, and the knowledge was hard, that his task had never been to undo what he had done, but to finish what he had begun . . . In silence, man and shadow met face to face, and stopped. Aloud and clearly, breaking that old silence, Ged spoke the shadow's name, and in the same moment the shadow spoke without lips or tongue, saying the same word: Ged. And the two voices were one voice.

Ursula Le Guin, *A Wizard of Earthsea*

INNER COACHING EXERCISE: LOOKING AT DEMONS

▶ Take time to be with yourself in a state of mindfulness. Without homing in on any specific demon or problem it causes, allow yourself to wonder how your life would become freer, more whole and more fulfilling if you found a new way to be with the demons that haunt you, however great or trivial.

▶ Be curious now about one of your demons. On the inside, say 'Hello' to it. Notice what happens.

▶ Pay attention to any changes in how things look, sound, feel, taste or smell on the inside.

▶ Come back and consider what questions you would like to ask this demon. Pick one or two.

▶ Resume a state of mindfulness and, having reconnected with the demon, ask your questions. Respect the responses you get.

Chapter Seven

Shaping Your Reality

L anguage is one of the most powerful tools available to us. It shapes our communication with ourselves just as much as it expresses and shapes our communication with others. *It ain't what you say; it's the way that you say it.*

You can become aware of its power and use it more effectively every day, through noticing how words and phrases are used, and how repeated patterns build up their effects over time. In particular, when you learn to use language more deliberately and precisely in a mindful and reflective state, it can help your Inner Coaching become more precisely targeted.

So Inner Coaching is something that takes place when you are mindful and attending to the full range of experiential information available to you. So just *how* do you go about communicating with yourself? In this chapter we're going to show you how essential this knowledge can be in helping you get the most value from your Inner Coaching, and we're going to offer you some guidelines for making your own internal conversations easy, enjoyable and productive.

Words that work

Just why would you need to think about how you communicate with yourself? Surely it's just a matter of saying what comes naturally? Or is it? In our experience, the language you use every day and the language of your other-than-conscious processing can be as subtly – or as markedly – different as one dialect of the same language is from another. And since you're using your everyday conscious processing to formulate the themes, questions and requests you want to raise in your Inner Coaching, it can really help to think things through and plan in advance how you're going to present them to yourself when you enter your special Inner Coaching state. Like everything else about Inner Coaching, it gets easier with practice to know how best to approach yourself, what kinds of wording might cause problems, and which will really enable you to tap into resources that are beyond your conscious, everyday abilities.

Different parts of your mind are specialised to work in different ways, so when you seek to make cross-connections between them, some 'translating' is needed. In this chapter we're going to give you some straightforward dos and don'ts that will help you make the communi-cation as easy, problem-free and effective as possible.

We've already indicated that you can pick up a lot of information kinaesthetically – that is, through your own physical reactions and responses. And for some people this form of sensory awareness will constitute much of their 'conversation' with themselves. However, in this chapter we're going to concentrate on exploring the specific power of words, and helping you become more effective and subtle in the way you use them with yourself.

There are two reasons for this. First, many people already communi-cate with themselves through their ongoing internal dialogue, and we want you to become more aware of how this affects you. We've already shown how internal dialogue can limit people in their everyday states: as you become aware of the power and resonance of language you'll be able to monitor its everyday effects more subtly and skilfully. Second, we want to ensure that you know how to use it specifically to help your Inner Coaching.

Reflection of reality

It's worth remembering that language gives us a way to describe reality, but because it is conceptual it can only ever approximate to what it describes. It stands in for the real world of objects, feelings, thoughts. Think of the shades of difference between the words 'joy', 'pleasure' and 'delight', or between 'irritation', 'rage' and 'anger'. If you look at these from one direction, they seem to label differences that exist 'out there'; but you could argue that in offering shades of meaning they also help to reinforce or even create them.

Becoming more aware of how language is used, and of the shades of meaning which we all manipulate so effortlessly all the time, gives you the power to deconstruct it, evaluate it and choose more freely how you will respond. For example, what others say to you, or in your hearing, has an impact on you. Often this will take place almost outside your awareness and sometimes quite without your consent. So it can be really helpful to train yourself to listen to the actual words themselves, not simply to their overall meaning. Often this will give you important clues as to how they are being used to shape the 'reality' you experience – or the 'reality' someone else wants you to experience.

The same process happens internally. We have conversations with ourselves many times a day: sometimes we don't even realise this is going on, but even when we do, we rarely pay attention to the language that's being used or the effects it has. We could say that the art of Inner Coaching involves becoming aware of unintentional internal conversations just as much as it does of developing intentional ones. Because when you do, you are in a position to have more internal influence – with yourself. And this can help you transform an automatic everyday process into one that's more often purposeful and productive.

If you remember that every part of yourself is processing and reacting to information all the time, the more you are sensitive to everyday signals from within, and the faster and more effortlessly you are able to switch from everyday states to Inner Coaching – even for just a few moments – the more you can benefit from your full range of skills and resources.

Let's take an example of how 'everyday' language use can have profound effects – simply because it works away beyond the immediate level of rational, conscious understanding. Malcolm had been brought up by his mother in considerable poverty, his father having died in an industrial accident when he was seven. From this early age, he got used to making do and doing without. He hardly thought about it. Hard work and thrift became automatic, so that even when he reached middle age and had a successful career and a good income, he rarely thought of treating himself or his family to anything beyond the essentials. As for extravagance – never! When his wife or his children wanted to splash out a bit, he'd tell them that they could *'make do with what they had'*, ask them to *'go without a bit longer'*, remind them that it was important to *'save for a rainy day'*. He wasn't aware of using these kinds of expressions – and certainly he had no idea that they were actually phrased as direct commands – *'Make do'*, *'Go without'*, *'Save'*. Malcolm was just saying what came naturally – but what came naturally was his mother's repeated injunctions.

During his childhood, these had ensured the family's survival, and they had become part of Malcolm's internal auditory environment – taken quite for granted. They had governed his own behaviour for years, and had never been updated to accommodate the changes in his financial situation. He had heard the statements as commands, he had repeated them to himself almost unconsciously to guide his own behaviour, and now he was passing them on to others – still in their original, and most powerful, form. Once Ian helped him realise how he was continuing to give himself an outdated message, Malcolm was able to change the way he thought – and spoke. He didn't become wildly extravagant as a result, but he did feel more able to splash out on occasion, and he and his family began to *enjoy* a better lifestyle.

Words have incredible power, both in themselves and in the way they're used. One reason for this is that when they're spoken, they gain the extra dimensions of meaning that are available through sound, because of tone, pace and volume. A friend of ours still shudders when he remembers one of his schoolteachers commenting very quietly and very coldly as he chattered away in a silent preparation lesson: *'Les, you're being very selfish.'* It wasn't just the words: the comment was certainly well targeted because the last thing Les wanted to be thought of as was selfish, but it was the cool, dispassionate, unarguable judgemental tone that really got the message across. In later life, the word 'selfish' always carried overtones of this experience, whether Les thought it himself or whether others used it to him. By contrast, a client of Ian's finds her own name, replayed in her head in the voice of her grandfather, incredibly comforting and affirming. It's the tone and pitch of his voice that does it for her – conveying the same depth of affection it did when she was little.

Internal dialogue

If you have ever felt put down, or affirmed, by others, it's worth becoming aware of just *how* they did that to you, and how much part was played by words and their delivery. Even more important is to recognise that you can – and probably do – have a similar effect on yourself. That's why we included internal dialogue among the Sirens in Chapter 5, because your inner conversations can prevent you from achieving your goals, or stunt the development of your full potential, just as effectively as anything other people can do to you. Or, on the other hand, your internal dialogue can support you and enhance your ability to be your best.

Internal dialogue can work both ways – it all depends on how you direct the power. Think of geothermal energy, bubbling and boiling away beneath the Earth's crust. It can emerge through fault lines as devastating earthquakes, through volcanoes as choking, destructive and engulfing lava – or be channelled to provide heat and light as it is in New Zealand and Iceland. In fact, Iceland's capital city, Reykjavik, is largely powered by geothermal energy. Language can have similarly extreme effects – but in this case you get to choose what they are.

In his exciting and important book *The Inner Game of Work,* the American coach Tim Gallwey said: 'A harmonious relationship with oneself requires an internal conversation based on as much clarity, trust and choice as possible.'

In our experience, those are pretty good goals to work towards. If you take the view that Inner Coaching is about building the strongest and most harmonious relationship with yourself that you can, one of the important benefits is that so much more of your energies and your resources become available to you in your dealings with others. It's like a ripple effect, spreading outwards to encompass everything you encounter. That's how important it can be to establish a good relationship with yourself – and language is at the heart of it.

The way words are used

In this section we'd like to introduce you to some language strategies that will help you in your dealings with others and with yourself. Becoming aware of how words operate requires you to pay a rather different kind of attention from the one you employ every day: you need to look at what the words *do* and *how* they do it rather than *what* they're about. Many people who are effective are naturally aware of this: they choose and use words for maximum impact, whether it's as helpers, educators, writers and communicators, healers or salespeople.

In everyday life, of course, we tend to pay more attention to the obvious content of words than to the way they work, which is one reason why so much of the influence words have is outside awareness. When you are just 'listening for meaning', you don't always tune in to the multi-layer message that's being simultaneously conveyed by the structure of the sentences, by what's implicitly assumed and what's ruled out, and by the audible dimensions of tone, volume, pitch and pace. Sometimes even when we do actually 'get' these underlying messages we are inclined to negate them by saying things like 'I'm sure she didn't really mean it like that.' Yet people's choices will often be governed not just by conscious intent but also by their unconscious attitudes and feelings. So what they say often *is* what they really mean.

It's these extra layers of meaning that are influential, because they have a direct impact on your state. States can be triggered by tone, by shades of possible meaning, by what's left out as well as what's said. This is important because the state you're in affects your behaviour, what you are able or not able to do, what you think and believe and in some cases your very sense of identity. Premature babies that are frequently stroked grow more and faster than ones that receive minimal touch. Words and their meanings can be a kind of auditory stroke which by its degree of frequency helps – or hinders – your emotional growth. Sometimes they are as important as that. And that's the case whether they are directed at you by someone else, or whether you are using them to yourself.

Things to look out for

- Notice how much you currently talk to yourself on the inside.

- What patterns does your self-talk have? Do you talk to yourself when things are going well, or only when things are going badly?

- What effects is your self-talk having? Does it open up new options? Or close them down? How does it leave you feeling?

Are we asking you to become an expert linguist before you can successfully engage in Inner Coaching? Yes – and no. You already *are* an expert linguist. Even the smallest child is sensitive to many of the shades of meaning we're talking about here. All we're asking you to do is to become more attentive to what you know already – and to use it to enhance the scope and effectiveness of your Inner Coaching.

Let's examine some key elements of language which are relevant here. In selecting these, we're drawing upon the language patterns of outstanding communicators that were identified during the early formulation of Neuro-Linguistic Programming (NLP). So if you already know about NLP or about the hypnotic work of Milton Erickson, you'll recognise them. (If you want to know more about them, and about NLP, you could look at one of our other books, *The NLP Coach*.)

Each of these patterns affects the hearer at more than just the level of obvious content. It 'means' more than it 'says'. And even when you know how it works, and use it deliberately in your Inner Coaching sessions with yourself – *it still works*! Words are never neutral – so we might as well make sure they're loaded in our favour.

1. Framing

Just as the colour, thickness and decoration of a picture frame draws the viewer's attention to some aspects of the picture it contains at the expense of others, the structure of a sentence selectively draws your attention to some parts of the information it contains. Usually, it's the beginning of a sentence that 'sets things up'. Think of the difference in how you feel about a request that begins '*I don't suppose you could ...*', one that starts '*I wonder if you'd be so kind as to ...*' and yet another that begins '*Please would you ...*'. Each signals a different shade of meaning – even before you have heard the request itself! Or think of the difference in how you feel when someone starts off '*I've got to tell you that ...*, as opposed to '*I thought you'd like to hear that ...*' or '*I must say that ...*'.

Whether you are talking to others or talking to yourself, it makes a big difference how you 'signal' what's coming. Trying to solve a *problem* is very different from working towards an *outcome*, whether you're asking for external or internal help in making the changes involved. We're not saying that one or the other is automatically better or worse

– simply that the framing draws attention to different aspects of the situation and sets the listener up to respond differently.

At first it can seem strange to think in advance about how you are going to frame something – to *yourself*. But remember, when you're doing Inner Coaching some parts of you are listening. Be mindful of how 'you' and your requests are going to come across to them.

INNER COACHING TIP: FRAMING FOR OUTCOMES

▶ It can really make a difference to your relationship with yourself to frame things as outcomes rather than problems, and to be courteous rather than dictatorial. For example, it's better to say/think, '*I'd really like some help in finding ways to get thinner*' rather than '*Do something about me being so fat.*' And better to say, '*I'd be really pleased if you could improve my relationship with my boss*' rather than '*Make sure I keep my temper when I next see him.*'

---

2. Presuppositions

Framing presupposes that something is more important than something else – then it draws your attention that way. There are also one-word presuppositions that are just as powerful. Think of the words 'but' and 'though'. Even in your inner conversations, you can easily negate something positive by adding one of these! '*I did really well at that, **though** my boss would have done it better*' or '*I'm really pleased that I've finished that on time – **but** of course there's still loads more to do.*' Doesn't feel too brilliant, does it? You're giving to yourself with one hand and taking away with the other. The presupposition (that you could have done better) is buried in the little word that links one half of the sentence to the other.

Let's take a word that works the other way. '*I haven't got the hang of this software – yet*'. 'Yet' is a really empowering little word, because it presupposes that there will be a time when you do. '*I can't give a presentation without feeling shaky and anxious – **yet**.*' Comforting? Encouraging? It acknowledges the problem you're having – but then it reminds you that this doesn't have to be the case for ever.

┌─── **INNER COACHING TIPS: DON'T SUPPOSE ...** ───┐

▶ Monitor how you and others use these little connecting words in everyday speech – and what effects they have. Then deliberately set out to use them for positive effect.

▶ When you think about how you're going to raise an issue with yourself in Inner Coaching, make sure that what your language presupposes will help rather than hinder you.

└───┘

3. Embedded commands

Remember how Malcolm's internal dialogue about spending and saving was full of injunctions based on his mother's experience of managing poverty? These came in the form of commands – but they were partly disguised because they were buried in the middles of sentences. These are common in everyday language. '*Make sure you don't miss the bus*' seems to be telling you to be sure to catch the bus, but if you look closely there's a command embedded in the sentence. And it turns the meaning of the sentence on its head – '*Miss the bus*'! For this reason these structures are called 'embedded commands'.

Embedded commands have a specific effect on the unconscious mind. The great American hypnotherapist Milton Erickson recognised through years of clinical experience that the unconscious part of the mind is very literal in the way it understands and responds to language. It will hear the command element even if it is embedded, and may well accept it as an instruction to act. However, to make sense of negatives – in order to understand what it shouldn't do – the unconscious mind has first to grasp the idea of doing it. What shouldn't I do? – *miss the bus*. So a sentence like this will at the very least be confusing to the hearer, and might even have the hidden effect of giving the opposite instruction to what's intended.

You can sometimes see this process graphically demonstrated by children. Ian remembers a grandmother telling her grandson, 'Now careful you don't slip on the polished floor.' The next moment that's exactly what he'd done. Like everything else, though, embedded commands have their uses. One time when he couldn't go to sleep, Ian began running an internal monologue that went: '*It may not be* *possible to **begin to relax right now**. But even though you are not **feeling sleepy right now** ...'* And as he continued he did indeed relax and fall asleep.

The conscious part of your mind works differently: it doesn't have a problem with negatives, and it can handle symbols and metaphors easily. This is why negatives aren't a problem for it. It hears the 'don't' and takes what comes next as a cancel.

Why do things like this matter? Well, when you allow yourself to enter a reflective, mindful state you are bringing more of your mind – specifically, your unconscious processing – on line. You're creating the opportunity for Inner Coaching. Yet the very bit of your mind you're seeking to connect with more freely and extensively is the bit that is most aware of these kinds of subtleties and most affected by them. You want to make your Inner Coaching as fluent and effective as possible, so you need a way to minimise these potentially limiting effects that one of your key means of communication – language – can have. Even though you know, consciously, what you're doing, you will hear the buried command differently when you are in a mindful state – because you will be attending to it at an unconscious level.

INNER COACHING TIPS: HIDDEN MESSAGES

▶ In everyday conversation, listen out for injunctions that could act as embedded commands. You need to be alert for two things: 1) the commanding form of the verb, often buried in a generalised statement or observation, which is potentially telling someone to do something (for example, *'I understand that you'd rather go out and play with your friends than **tidy your room**'*) and 2) a shift in voice tone or emphasis, or a pause before a word, which marks it out in some way (such as, *'It's not always easy to ... **find time** to tidy your room'*).

▶ Seek out opportunities for conveying your wishes to others in this indirect way.

▶ When you have something important to consider with yourself in your Inner Coaching, think about using embedded commands to make it easier for yourself to give – and receive – the desired message.

4. Portmanteau words

Language often stands in for experience: it acts as a symbol for it. Sometimes it's a kind of shorthand for pretty complex experiences. Take 'love', 'jealousy', 'enthusiasm', 'dedication' or 'laziness'. It's very easy to assume when someone uses one of these words in conversation that you know what they mean. Yet to one person, 'love' means being accepted warts and all, to another it means being looked after attentively and to yet another it may evoke intense physical passion.

It's relatively easy to accept that an abstract word of this kind, which stands for a complex constellation of experiences and meanings, could mean different things to different people. But how could such a word be a problem when it's only you who is involved? *Knowing what specifically is meant* is the issue in both cases.

It's natural to expect that being more available to yourself might help you move more surely and effectively towards your goals. And indeed it can. But suppose your goal is *'I want to be **happy**'*, or *'I want this project to **succeed**'*. What do these words really mean for you? If you don't know specifically, how can you find your course, or be sure that you're keeping to it? How will you know when you're happy? What will tell you that the project is a success?

If you were asking a friend to help you achieve something, you'd try to make it clear just what you wanted. *'Could you give me a hand painting the kitchen next weekend?'* *'Would you give me a lift in to work on Friday?'* Think of your inner self as a friend, and you'll see the value of being specific even to yourself. You could well benefit from your unconscious ability to monitor the passage of time, so asking yourself for help in waking up in time to catch that early train could be a good idea. You might be able to find some extra energy to get you through a crisis, if you ask courteously and promise yourself some time off afterwards. But 'happiness' – how? You need to be specific.

INNER COACHING TIPS: LOADED WITH MEANING?

▶ Listen out for portmanteau words in ordinary conversation, in the newspapers and on television. Where you can, try to find out just what they mean to the person using them.

> ▶ Get used to monitoring your own use of them.
>
> ▶ Use your Inner Coaching to explore just what is involved, for you, in a word that's important to you: 'love', 'loyalty', 'honesty', 'responsibility', 'friendship', 'caring' are some examples of portmanteau words that can have important, yet different, connotations for different people.
>
> ▶ Where you think that different meanings for a portmanteau word may be causing problems in a personal or work relationship, discuss them with the other person.
>
> ▶ Use your Inner Coaching to explore what it might be like if the word meant that for you. How would you feel, think and act? Ask yourself if this gives you any pointers for improving the way you relate to that person.

5. Search words

Now that you're aware of these portmanteau words, we want to highlight how you can sometimes put them to use as search engines. Vague or abstract words can be really helpful if you feel stuck or not very resourceful. They can prompt you to search for meaning, because their very lack of specificity will engage your other-than-conscious processing. When it's confronted with nonspecific words it simply has to search for content! As it does so, it's more likely to come up with things your conscious, logical thinking had so far missed. This can be a help in accessing your ability to make creative connections and solve problems at an unconscious level.

Often, portmanteau words can act like this, if you're using them in a searching way. For example, *'I'd like to feel more fulfilled'* can engage your inner wisdom in a very open way: the word 'fulfilled' doesn't have specific content – though it certainly has meanings for you – so you'll have to search to find just what might help you achieve it.

Wendy remembers having to organise her daughter Charlotte's seventh birthday party. Wendy was not that enthusiastic about holding a party for small children, and kept putting off thinking about what might keep the children occupied and happy (that word again!). The day came closer . . . and closer. Eventually she realised she simply had to plan something. So she put herself into a mindful state and asked herself: *'What would be a **fun thing** for the children to do to keep them **occupied and happy** at Charlotte's party?'* The answer came quick as a flash: *'Plates'*. Wendy would provide each child with a plain white plate which they could decorate with glazes from a neighbour who was a potter. Designing and painting the plates would keep the children happily occupied, and a week later each one would get a present which they themselves had made.

Language can be a key to unlocking inner possibilities. Wendy already had all the essential information she needed – but she hadn't put it together until she asked *'What would be a fun thing for the children to do?'* The words 'fun', occupied' and 'happy' stimulated an inner search and a creative linking, which brought together the ideas of plates, glazes and her neighbour.

Imagine that instead of a relatively minor need like this one the issue was life-threatening, or the situation called for thinking 'outside the box'. What if you were unhappy in your job – or your relationship – and didn't know what to do for the best? This could well be a time to use words like 'happier', 'more fulfilled', 'more rewarded' and 'stretched' in your Inner Coaching.

INNER COACHING TIPS: LEADING THE SEARCH

▶ Begin to notice and collect search words in ordinary conversation.

▶ Consider how you could use portmanteau words to stimulate inner searching.

▶ Rehearse some actual phrases you might use in Inner Coaching to help you gain access to options and solutions you haven't yet been able to think of consciously.

▶ Then begin to incorporate them into your Inner Coaching sessions.

6. Metaphors

Our everyday language is rich in metaphor. Similes and metaphors express what we mean by analogy, through finding likenesses which illuminate what we're talking about. From one-word expressions like 'bullish' through to more elaborate comparisons like 'bright as a button' and even running images that come to characterise an individual through repetition – like those of conflict in Mrs Thatcher's speeches – metaphors give life and variety to language. Common phrases are also often metaphoric: *get a grip on that, blind to what was going on, deaf to the world.* The more frequently they are used, the less we register that they're actually metaphors.

It's important to become aware of metaphors when you're doing Inner Coaching, because of the literal way that unconscious processing works. As you think consciously about what you want to say to yourself, you might well be using metaphoric language. But your unconscious won't take it metaphorically! People sometimes say of someone very successful in business that 'everything they touch turns to gold'. But that's very different from what happened to King Midas. Midas asked the gods to make everything he touched turn to gold. And that was exactly what happened – *everything* he touched, including his wife and family, became solid gold. Like the unconscious, the gods had taken his request literally.

There's a Chinese proverb: *Be careful what you ask for – you may get it.* Whether you ask yourself deliberately or just focus your attention repeatedly and intensely on what you want, setting your mind on something often has a way of making it happen. And that's because when you put the object of your focus right in the centre of your awareness you end up aiming your actions, as well as your thinking, towards it – whether it's something you want or something you dread.

For a practical illustration of this, try staring at one side of the pavement or path as you walk along and notice how you just seem to drift over to that side. In the same way, a driving instructor we know told us how many of his students would steer by the white line in the centre of the road – and end up drifting too far over.

So it's important for you to make sure that what you ask for is what you *really* want – whether you're asking in your mindful times with yourself or whether you're simply caught up in anxiety about illness, failure or disaster.

INNER COACHING TIPS: SPOTTING THE METAPHOR

▶ When you have a request in mind, whether it's for an inner search or for help in achieving something specific, check out the language you're using. Are any metaphors involved? Is it ambiguous?

▶ If necessary, rephrase it – more than once if you have to – until you're sure your wording really does say what you want, clearly and unambiguously. It really is worth your while to do this before beginning your inner work.

Inner Coaching is a powerful process, and its power can be greatly enhanced – or lessened – by the language you use to do it. As you use our tips to help you become more alert to the effects language has in the everyday world, you'll find yourself becoming more effective in using it, and so more influential in your relationships at work and play. Learning what your own automatic patterns of speech are doing to you or for you can be enormously enabling. Once you know the patterns that limit, you begin to catch yourself as you use them – or soon after, and you can build your skill in subtle variations and amendments that get you nearer to what you really want to say. And once you know how your self-communication can enhance your well-being and effectiveness, you can deliberately make more use of the patterns that work for you. Change the language, and you really do change the reality of your experience.

The way that you tell it - your story your way

So far in this chapter we've been talking about the specifics of language. Now we want to broaden the focus and consider how it can be cumulative in its effects. In particular, let's look at the way you talk to yourself about you – the way you think about yourself and tell the stories of your life. And we want to explore how this apparently anecdotal storytelling can in fact end up shaping what comes next. Because who's listening every time the stories are told? You are.

We've shown how special and distinct the Inner Coaching process can be: when you deliberately take yourself into an Inner Coaching state, you know you're bringing so much more of yourself on-line. But in this chapter we've also shown how the resonances and ambiguities of language can get past your conscious scanning for meaning and create effects – sometimes quite profound ones – at other levels. We want to look at the way you – and others around you – create and maintain the story of your life and what's significant about it. Anecdotes and family opinions can impact every layer of your being – for good or ill. So it's useful to become aware of just how you and others repeatedly refer to you, and what overall impact this may be having. You can explore this in Inner Coaching, and you can also use Inner Coaching to address any problems that arise from it.

What do we mean by your story? When you think of yourself and your life experience, and when you talk to others about yourself, you have to select. It wouldn't be possible to refer to every event – you have to generalise. 'My parents were always there for me' sums up hundreds, probably even thousands, of individual actions and events (and of course 'there for me' is also a portmanteau phrase). When you say, 'I was the outsider at school' or 'I was the baby of the family' or 'My dad was a bit of a cowboy,' you're telling a story – and as you tell the story, you reinforce it.

Most people have anecdotes that come out from time to time. How your little brother offended your great-aunt when he innocently asked: 'Auntie, why is your skin like orange peel?' How your grand-dad kept everything – but *everything* – so that if any of the family or the neighbours ever needed a left-handed widget he was bound to have one … Sometimes these stories are about particular events; sometimes they're about individuals' characteristic habits. Sometimes they're amusing or affectionate, sometimes embarrassing. Every time they're told, they help create a kind of mould that sets the character of the person or the event. Events, good and bad, get codified like this too – have you ever noticed how you tend to use the same phrases each time? 'And then this other car just came round that corner and I thought "I'm a goner".'

The way you tell the story frames its meaning – and shapes you in the process. Your brother may squirm at that story revealing his infant outspokenness – but does he perhaps continue to think of himself as blunt and direct? You actually survived that accident: does the way you describe that moment of apparent finality make you live your ongoing life with gratitude, optimism and a sense of escape? Your dad was indeed a bit of a cowboy – but what about his sensitivity when you were ill? These stories highlight some things, but they can leave out others which may be important or beneficial.

Think of the way you see your life as a whole. Is it a rags-to-riches story? Is it a poor-me story of exploitation and victimisation? Is it a survival-against-the-odds story? All of these narratives have a funda-mental link to the 'truth' of your experience, both in terms of events and in terms of the meanings you and those close to you have made of them. But they are more powerful than that. In effect, they can act as a powerful means whereby the past shapes the present and the future in its own likeness. They can be self-fulfilling. Is this story the one that helps you the most in life?

Even 'good' narratives can be limiting – just because in their taken-for-granted state they may be ruling out other possibilities. Think of the 'good' little boy who is praised for looking after his mother when his dad dies, who takes pride in his self-sufficiency and caring role – and may or may not realise that he doesn't have to be the provider and carer for ever. It's not for others to say this is limiting; but we've encountered clients who did suddenly realise that they wanted more from life than the well-established, successful and well-rewarded role they'd acquired earlier in life.

How can you use Inner Coaching to help you with your life story? Potentially, reflecting on it and working with it in that special state of openness and inner availability can help you find and reinforce enabling truths, feel more empowered, signal undiscovered potential, help reconnect you with experiences and goals you've lost sight of ... The possibilities are endless.

As you reflect on your life, and the meanings you have made of it, do so with the intention of becoming open to new understanding. A student of Ian's who did this said afterwards, in a tone of surprise and disappointment, 'I thought my childhood was much worse than that.' For her, the exercise revealed good experiences that had been over-looked, because the story she told herself had been formed at a time when she was indeed unhappy. The strength of these feelings had made her filter out conflicting 'evidence', and the unhappy saga had then set. Only her willingness to revisit it allowed her to regain so much that had been lost. She had to 'rewrite' and forgo some of what she'd been accustomed to, of course; but in the process she freed herself for new options and new discoveries.

Sometimes 'rewriting history' like this isn't easy. People who have been victims often find it very difficult to let go of the hard-luck story and the identity that goes along with it, yet it's an essential step if they are to move out of their victim role. 'Conmen always seem to see me coming,' said one much-exploited client, resigned to a lifetime of further exploitation. For her, the alternative scenario – one of self-assertion and increased self-worth – also meant that she had to face her anger at being duped so many times. She had to forgive herself, and let go the experiences that had taught her to be so gullible.

Another client found her personal 'updating' a much easier experience. Her sister had been killed in a road accident, and she had blocked out all memories before the accident and grown up with a strong belief that she was 'the wrong sister'. This in turn set the tone for a difficult relationship with her parents. Only in middle age, when she revisited some of her early experiences, did she recover everyday memories of an averagely happy childhood, in which she had been accepted equally and valued even though she was very different from her sister. As she started to tell herself a new version of her childhood, her life story began to change – and so did her life. There was more confidence, a growing ease with being who she was, and much less of the feeling that she was 'the wrong sister'. And this began to change how she behaved towards her parents – which in turn affected how they behaved towards her. Over time, the relationship was transformed.

INNER COACHING TIPS: FINDING THE PLOT

▶ Become aware of the effect your current narrative of your life may be having on how you handle your present experiences and anticipate what is to come. Is this how you want to shape your world? If not, use your Inner Coaching to begin searching for other ways to think and to respond.

▶ Consider how you'd like your narrative to go in future. For many people, changing the pattern involves honouring their younger selves, even if they made mistakes or adopted patterns of thought or behaviour that they now find limiting or disapprove of. It can also mean coming to understand how their history has helped shape their identity, and how they may quite unintentionally be continuing to perpetuate just what dissatisfies them. Then it becomes possible, if they wish, to begin learning some new ways of interacting with others. What kind of story do you want to be telling tomorrow, next year, in ten years' time? Use your Inner Coaching both to help you construct the kind of story that will enhance your life, and to monitor and if necessary amend it on an ongoing basis.

In our experience, it's worth thinking about how you engage with yourself, and even worth trying out a number of versions before you enter your mindful coaching state. And that's because you want your communication with you to be fresh, sharp, clear, economical – and effective. You want to get your message across. You also need to become aware of how language is currently shaping your experience, so that you can decide if this is how you want your personal narrative to be told.

INNER COACHING EXERCISE: EXPLORE YOUR STORY

▶ Allow yourself to become mindful of words that have been potent in your family and your history. If you do this in a mindful state you are likely to add information to what you already 'know' you know.

▶ Notice their resonances and the shaping effects they have had. Are you comfortable with these effects, or do you want to change them in the future?

▶ Experiment with telling yourself different versions of your story. Start with the 'old, old story' as you've always told it. Than play with different versions. What's it like hammed up as Hollywood? What's it like as a musical? Suppose you and it were together to become a 'living legend'? Is it perhaps a tragedy that can 'purge the mind of pity and terror' like the classical tragedies? Are you indeed the central figure? How does it feel if you are – and if you aren't? And how does it feel to change? The object is not to choose a new format and let your story become set in it, but rather to explore it in a way which is playful and creative while wholly respectful of facts and feelings. How do you want your story to go?

> ▶ Notice how you feel in response to each version of your story. Do you feel more – or less – comfortable, more or less empowered as you 'try it on for size'? How does it affect your view of the future?

In this chapter we've been exploring one of the core ingredients of Inner Coaching – language and how you use it. We've been inviting you to become more aware of language in everyday life, recognising that this is one end of a continuum of experience along which you can move easily and naturally and that incorporates that more inward and mindful state which we call Inner Coaching. As you become more sensitive to your frequent changes of state along the continuum, and more aware of how you and others are using language, you'll find it easier to use it to shape the reality you want, rather than having to put up with the realities you don't want. In the next chapter we're going to look at one very specific use of language which plays a key part in all forms of coaching, including Inner Coaching. And that is asking questions.

Chapter Eight

Asking the Right Questions

The root of the word 'question', and its relative 'quest', is the Latin *quaestio*, which means 'search'. And searching is at the heart of all forms of coaching, especially Inner Coaching. That's because all coaching specifically seeks to help you go beyond what you already know, understand or can do: it's a process that facilitates *learning* and *growth*. What's special about Inner Coaching, of course, is that it connects you directly with so many resources, and so much mind-body information, that's not normally available in everyday consciousness. So when you ask questions in your Inner Coaching state, you can benefit even more.

There's an art to asking the right questions in the right way. This is partly a matter of language, as the previous chapter showed. But it's also to do with how tightly you frame the question. If you ask a really specific question, you're framing your inner search to seek a really specific answer. And this may limit what you're able to come up with. If you ask a more open question, you're allowing and encouraging your other-than-conscious mind to broaden the scope of its inquiries. We're going to show you how you can frame questions that help you get the kinds of answers you need.

Questioning can go two ways. You can consciously formulate a question for your other-than-conscious self, and you can also learn to take note of information that reaches your conscious awareness through your body, through intuitions, gut feelings or dreams. And we also find it useful to assume that the communications you receive *from* your body or your unconscious may be questions *for* your conscious mind. Changes in your feelings of physical well-being, for example, may be questioning your patterns of exercise, eating habits or work-life balance. 'Gut feelings', both positive and negative, may be a way of questioning your automatic responses to other people or to life experiences, as we'll explore more fully in Chapter 11.

Either way, questioning is a means of focusing on things that are relevant and important and can help you explore them. So questioning yourself is a way to begin a process of exploration and discovery that can profoundly change the way you understand things, the way you operate and the way you feel.

When to ask questions of yourself

It's likely that many people will first think of asking questions when they're in trouble and need specific help. They want something to stop, or to change for the better. Or perhaps they'll think of asking when they want to make a special effort to achieve a particular goal. This is natural, but it's limited and can also be limiting. In our experience it's much more useful to develop a habit of self-questioning on a regular basis, whether or not you're aware of a specific reason. It's almost like making a regular time to go off inside and say to yourself, *'How am I doing?'* And that's like an invitation to do a bit of internal stocktaking. There could be all kinds of possible responses. Matters of physical well-being or comfort, odd niggles of mind or body, interpersonal concerns, issues that really need addressing now or that may be important in helping you find your future path or stay on track for your chosen quest. All of these could come to your attention as a result of such an open invitation for self-awareness and self-evaluation.

Formulating questions for Inner Coaching

To ask a question is to imply that the recipient of the question has relevant information and is in a position to supply it. And indeed, experience shows that both your other-than-conscious mind and your body do have information which can be accessed in this way. But the information you can get depends on the kind of question you ask and the way you ask it.

1. Tight questions – tight answers

It's perfectly possible to limit the information your body or your unconscious can deliver if you only ask the kind of question that elicits a 'yes' or a 'no', or perhaps just adds information to what you already have. This is not to deny the value of asking yourself questions like: *'What was the name of that man in accounts I was introduced to at the meeting?'*, *'Just when was it that I last had the car serviced?'* or *'How could I reorganise my office to make the most of the available space?'* Asking such questions in a mindful state may well initiate a search that produces the answers you wanted, either immediately or after some time. But the answer has been framed, and therefore limited, by the form of the question. It's as though you've invited your other-than-conscious mind to fill in the gaps, as becomes clear if you turn the questions around. Essentially, they're statements:

'The name of the man I was introduced to at the meeting was . . .'

'I last had the car serviced in . . .'

'I could reorganise my office to make it seem more spacious by . . .'

Inner Coaching can deliver this kind of information, of course, but it's our intention in this chapter to show you how very much more it can also do!

2. Open questions – wider access

These are the kinds of questions to ask when you really don't know the answer, ones that put you in touch with 'the parts that other questions can't reach'; and they're deliberately framed in such a way as to allow many different possible answers. You want to give yourself permission for as extensive a search as it takes.

An open question can begin with phrases like:

'I wonder why...?'

'How does it come about that...?'

'What might be the reason/benefit of this . . . ?'

'What's the underlying link between . . . ?'

'Is there a way in which I could . . .'

'Was there ever a time when . . . ?'

'What might be the first steps towards . . . ?'

Though the conscious 'you' doesn't know the answers, it's surprising how often Inner Coaching can help you find them. And that's because each of us has so much information stored outside of consciousness, including much that concerns the workings of the body and the links between 'body' and 'mind'.

INNER COACHING TIPS: SHAPING QUESTIONS

▶ Start noticing times when you wonder about your patterns of feeling or behaviour in everyday life. Maybe keep a notebook handy to jot them down.

▶ When you have a quiet moment, frame some of these queries into questions that you can pose to yourself in Inner Coaching, using some of the patterns we have given above.

▶ Incorporate one of these questions into your next Inner Coaching time.

The questions we listed all prompt a search for reasons, and our experience shows that you can get a long way with them. But there's another kind of question which can be even more rewarding. It provokes wondering then action and it often takes a different form. Here are some examples.

'I wonder if I could begin to . . .'

'I'd really like to find a way to . . .'

'It would really help if I knew more about . . .'

'I wonder when I might discover how to . . .'

'I'd really appreciate it if my inner healer/unconscious mind would help me to . . .'

Statements like these pose a question of a different kind to your inner processing. *Can you? When will you? Could you please?* In essence, they all say, *'Can you help?'* And they all make it clear that you believe that help is possible, and that it would be valued.

There's another payoff to asking questions like this. The bit that you fill in after the . . . in each of these questions is going to act as an embedded command, just because of the way it has to be worded. If you begin with *'I'd really like to find a way to . . .'* you're going to continue with a verb: *do this, know more about, feel more/less, understand,* and so on. You're giving yourself an instruction – but in the most open and permissive way. If it feels difficult at first to formulate this kind of question, we can assure you that the more you practise, the easier and more natural it gets. And it can only produce beneficial outcomes. This form of inner questioning really is loaded for success!

INNER COACHING EXERCISE: RAISING ISSUES

▶ Take an issue or problem that concerns you. Experiment with different examples of phrasing from our list to find the way of wording it that best seems to fit you. Write down alternatives if it helps.

▶ Use your chosen format to raise the question with yourself in your Inner Coaching.

Receiving answers

How do you know when your question has been answered? Sometimes when you take yourself into a mindful state – whether it's for a few moments or for the 20-minute break that we talked about earlier – and ask yourself questions, you'll get a more or less instant response. It's as though you're getting a brief – often pictorial or one-word – reply. *'Walking and gardening'* you'll think, in response to the perennial *'How can I get fitter?'* question. When you're feeling rundown after flu, *'Brazil nuts'* may suddenly surface from an article you read ages ago about the value of selenium in boosting the immune system. Or maybe, like a friend of ours, you just find yourself remembering how good Brazil nuts taste and choosing to have a few as a daily midmorning snack. Imagine her surprise when she subsequently discovered how much good they were doing her! Her body knew before her mind.

Noticing things that somehow hadn't caught your attention before is another way information may reach you from the unconscious. You're feeling bored and in need of stimulation; you ask yourself what to do; suddenly you keep seeing articles and hearing snippets on the radio about working holidays. The information has obviously been potentially available all the time, yet suddenly it's begun standing out for you – because you needed it and asked.

While we've tended to describe Inner Coaching as an encounter or even a conversation, it's clear that the responses you get from your other-than-conscious mind or from your body don't always come in the same forms as those you use consciously. In response to your enquiry, you might get an image or even a physical response. (Think of how eloquently your heart can sink, your stomach churn or your head feel faint in response to memories, events or suggestions for the future.) If language is the means, often it's a short telegraphic phrase or even just a single word rather than a fully elaborated thought.

In our experience, it's this kind of condensed or symbolic response that tells you the answer is truly coming from some inner part of yourself, whether it occurs while you're still in a mindful state or whether it comes to you later. It's likely that you'll feel some kind of confirming response: *'Aha!', 'Oh shit!', 'Of course!'* or *'Why didn't I think of that sooner?'* Sometimes you might feel amused, or alternatively puzzled because you sense that it's right but can't quite see how. It's rather like finding the missing piece of the jigsaw puzzle – you have a sense of completion and relief. Take a moment to think back and find examples from your own experience.

Not every answer comes at once, or in an obvious form. Ian was a teenager at the time when pirate radios were starting up. They had immense attraction for him and many other young people because they were lively and innovative, spoke directly to the young, and broke the mould of established radio. As a teenager, Ian really wanted to be out there on the North Sea reaching a generation, creating a new kind of culture and giving the audience a different kind of experience. It never happened. Pirate radio came ashore, and Ian grew up. Clearly, things didn't turn out the way he'd hoped. But is that really true? Nowadays Ian has an international training organisation and reaches thousands of people through his training, his books and his broadcasting. As a coach he has the satisfaction of knowing that he is supporting his clients in creating the changes they are seeking. Ian's teenage ambition was realised after all, in a way that he could never have imagined. That's why he often says, 'Honour the purpose. Don't get hooked on the form'.

Great questions

We've shown how 'wondering' or search questions can connect you to a wealth of information you didn't know you had. Among these we've found some specific ones which can be particularly powerful, and we'd like to show you in more detail just how they work. They are great questions in any kind of coaching – but with Inner Coaching their access is deeper and more immediate.

When you want to do something and yet just can't seem to, it's worth asking yourself one – or both – of the following questions:

'What stops me?'

'What would happen if I did?'

These both get you searching for reasons and payoffs underlying your current behaviour. We've found it's useful to assume that there's a self-caring intention behind everything we do or don't do, however strange or self-destructive it may seem. Seeking the reason directs our search towards the consequences we are, probably unconsciously, anticipating. You'll find that most times you ask these questions the answer comes back straight away – you knew what the block was even though you didn't know you knew. And once you have the information, you can factor it in and find more constructive ways of achieving the same ends.

A common example is wanting to give up a 'bad' habit. On the surface, it seems obvious that it would be better to quit – yet somehow you just don't. When you ask these questions, you may find that the habit is serving you as a form of treat, or a rest, or a celebration. In a nutshell, it's an attempt at self-care. When people reach this point, they often start pondering about how much care they really get in their lives, whether they take enough time off and whether they are valued enough by others. Sometimes this brings uncomfortable or even painful awareness about how off-balance their lives are. But even so it allows them to make a more informed choice, so that they can find better ways of self-nurturing.

Another really good question is: *'What's going on here?'* When feelings are running high, when reactions to what's happening seem puzzling or out of proportion, it's usually because something important is being touched on or even threatened, even if you or others don't realise it. Often, this cues you in to what the hidden issues really are.

When you make a rapid judgement about something or someone, it's worth asking yourself, *'What tells me that this is so?'* This question sends you on a search for evidence. Often, we do make judgements at an unconscious level, and may lack the confidence to speak them aloud or act on them if we haven't 'caught up with the evidence' consciously. If you are reluctant to do something that's proposed, or feel you are holding back from trusting a situation or a person, yet can't find the reasons, remind yourself that there *is* always some evidence somewhere, because that's what's causing the reluctance. Asking the question helps put you in touch with the information you need.

There's a related question that can help you with the future. When you're aiming for something or wanting something to be a certain way, take the time to ask yourself, *'How would I know?'* (We talked about this in relation to ideas like 'happiness' and 'success' earlier.) In responding to this question, Inner Coaching will usually be able to tell you what specific evidence you need.

When seeking help from within in making a choice or solving a problem, don't be content with the first answer that comes, however brilliant it seems. There will be more where that came from! Ask yourself, *'What else?'* You are capable of making many innovative connections; give yourself time to go on working. Often the second or third idea may be better still.

Next comes a question that can feel challenging, but that can help you make major shifts in thinking, feeling and behaviour just because it is. You may be feeling under the weather, hard done by, let down, disappointed, exploited or hurt. Respectfully, calmly, thoughtfully ask yourself, *'So what now?'* Your tone acknowledges the emotional tenor of the situation: it *is* tough right now. But your question takes you forward, because it requires you to focus on what comes next. It implies *'And what am I going to do about that?'* By shifting your attention from how you *feel* to how you're going to *act*, it reminds you that right now you do have a choice. So it empowers you by connecting you with your own inner resourcefulness.

And finally, one of the most vital coaching questions of all: *'What do*

I really want?' Often people are motivated by what they think they want, what they ought to want or what others want them to want. Asking the 'really want' question in a state of mindfulness is a way of touching base with yourself. And the answers that come will often surprise you.

Knowing what you really want doesn't mean that's what you *have* to do. You still have the choice to put others first, or to defer your ultimate goal because something else is urgent or important in the short-term. But what it does mean is that you act in knowledge of your inner wishes and with the possibility of reaching some agreement between your differing, or even conflicting, impulses. Not all your choices will be easy, but knowing your baseline means that you have more chance of being and acting in harmony with yourself.

Where's it all leading?

These are all great questions to ask yourself. There's another great question you can ask, and a special format for asking it so that it really gives you maximum information. The question is *'What would this give me?'* The format is sometimes referred to as laddering, because you keep repeating the same question, and each time it prompts a further answer, giving you a sequence that leads you onwards and upwards until you reach something really important to you.

A client of ours had looked forward for years to his retirement, relishing the prospect of spending more time with his wife, in his garden and on exotic holidays. But when the time came, it all seemed hollow and insubstantial, because he had never updated what this would mean to him once he had it.

The important step he had missed out was asking himself: *'What would retirement give me?'* When we asked him, the answer was, *'Freedom from the need to work.'* Though true, this only specified the *absence* of something he found burdensome, not the *presence* of anything.

So we put the same question to him again: *'What would freedom from the need to work give you?'* And he answered: *'The chance to spend my days as I choose.'* Asking again, *'And what would the chance to spend your days as you choose give you?'* produced the answer: *'The chance to fulfil my potential.'* *'And what would that give you?'* *'The sense that my life matters.'* As the sequence of questions progressed, it became clear why retirement was so disappointing to him: the mere absence of work failed to match up to his deep wish that his life should matter. Once this was unpacked, he was able to think again about what he really wanted for his retirement – and his life.

Let's recap the full sequence just as it happened:

'What would retirement give you?'

'Freedom from the need to work.'

'What would freedom from the need to work give you?'

'The chance to spend my days as I choose.'

'And what would the chance to spend your days as you choose give you?'

'The chance to fulfil my potential.'

'And what would that give you?'

'The sense that my life matters.'

Repeating the question like this in relation to the series of answers you get takes you further and further towards the heart of who you are and what you value most in life. Usually, as in our client's case, there comes a point when you know there just isn't a more significant answer left to give. And in the process you'll have learnt a lot about what matters to you, and what depths of meaning your ambitions and wishes, even quite 'ordinary' ones, may carry. Through questioning, you are steering yourself towards the heart of your personal quest in life. The process of search that a question begins can, as in this case, help you begin to find out more about an even bigger search – your personal search for meaning in life. We'll explore other ways in which Inner Coaching can help you with this greater search in Chapter 10.

Our client's quest was that he should matter. We have known people seeking *'to make a difference in the world'*, *'to help others become the best that they can be'*, *'to make a dent, however small, in suffering'*. Often, some sense of human connectedness and service is involved.

Surprisingly, the same may be true once you start to unpack more obviously worldly ambitions like *'earn enough to buy a bigger house'* or *'take a major cruise every year'*. Though at first these seem to be ends in themselves, often they serve deeper purposes like making life better for the family, discovering the world, and so on.

INNER COACHING EXERCISE: REFINING THE QUESTIONS

▶ Take one of your ambitions and use the laddering questions to ascertain its deeper purpose. Where did you get to? Now that you know what you hope it might ultimately achieve for you, are there any adjustments you want to make? Are there any other routes that will take you there faster, or more effectively?

▶ When your Inner Coaching doesn't seem to be delivering what you want, you don't need to give up in despair, or blame yourself for being inept. Instead, change the focus and ask yourself just what's creating the difficulty. Question yourself about your own questions: if an answer is not forthcoming, maybe you have asked the wrong question, or the right question in the wrong way ... Use Inner Coaching questions to help you find what you need to do next.

Questions from within

So far in this chapter we've concentrated on the kinds of questions you formulate consciously and use your Inner Coaching to explore with your other-than-conscious self. But sometimes our internal responses raise questions for *us*.

The classic example is messages from your body. We now know that body and mind are not separate entities, but rather interconnected systems. At microscopic levels electrical and chemical messengers transmit and receive instructions and make changes which can be experienced as physical, mental or emotional. So we now have a scientific explanation for what at some level people have known all along – that the body can often reflect what's going on in the mind.

A workaholic friend often tended to develop bouts of hay fever at weekends – but rarely during the week. Eventually he became aware of this as a pattern, and started to ask himself, *'What's this about?'* Thinking things over, he realised that during the week he was so driven by his sense of obligation that he pressured himself unreasonably. Come the weekend, just when he wanted to get jobs done in the house and around the garden, he had to retreat to the armchair or even to bed. It was as if his body-mind utilised his natural sensitivity to pollen to ensure that he took the time off that he needed to rest and recover.

You could say his body was trying to tell him something. He felt his body was posing a question: *'Is this the way you want to live your life?'* Once he recognised the pattern and began to unpack its meaning, he started to make changes in his working schedule to alleviate some of the pressure he had been allowing himself and others to impose. His allergic attacks began to dwindle in frequency and severity: he had 'heard' what his body was trying to tell him.

Other kinds of patterns may have similar messages. The compulsive patterns of eating, drinking, smoking or spending that bedevil many people's lives can often be taken as a message that life isn't fun enough, or sweet enough, or exciting enough, that the person feels they have to give themselves things because others ignore or exploit them – and so on. If you have a pattern that you find difficult to give up or cut down on, there's a good chance that it's serving some kind of life-enhancing or identity-nurturing purpose like this.

Dreams

We're going to consider dreams more fully in Chapter 11, because they're one way in which your unconscious intelligence helps you process your life experience, and a great everyday resource which is often neglected. So we only want to mention one of their functions here, which is that of prompting questions in consciousness.

We all know how powerful dreams can be. You can wake up with a sense of sadness, or exhilaration, and that feeling may stay with you for hours, or even most of the day. It's like you have to keep reminding yourself 'that was only a dream'. This can happen even when you don't remember what the dream was actually about. Rather than dismissing it, take the very strength of the feeling as an attempt to get through to you.

INNER COACHING EXERCISE: DREAMTIME

▶ When you next have a powerful dream, take some time to enter an Inner Coaching state. Recollect your dream and the feelings it brought up for you. Ask yourself if those feelings bring a question for you. Do they carry a suggestion, or a solution to a problem? Allow yourself to connect and wonder.

> ▶ If you have a recurrent dream, ask yourself in your Inner Coaching if it has unresolved questions for you to consider about your life now or in the past.

Questions lead you to answers. It's been said that there is only a finite number of plots in literature. There are probably only a few great questions in life. Ultimately, the great questions are about finding personal meaning and purpose. And we've seen in this chapter how rapidly a willingness to look at the smaller questions can take you to the bigger ones. Questioning can play a crucial role not just in gathering information but in uncovering motivation and creating direction in your life. Questioning isn't just the way you can elicit information from other-than-conscious parts of your body-mind: it's also the tool you can use to transform it into an active and energetic force for living more fully and more purposefully.

INNER COACHING EXERCISE: REFLECTIONS

> ▶ Take a few moments and allow yourself to enter a mindful state. Let yourself be the calm and accepting centre of your awareness. Check in. Ask yourself quietly, wonderingly, attentively, 'Well ...?'
>
> ▶ You might like to reflect on what the quest in your questions is. Is it worthy of you? And is it worth spending your life on? If not, how about asking some new questions?

Chapter Nine

Building an Inner Alliance

By now, you'll have got familiar with putting yourself into the state of openness and inner focus that facilitates Inner Coaching. And you have learned some of the tools you can use within it. You know about tuning in to your senses, about how the language you use shapes the reality of your experience and can help or hinder your Inner Coaching aims. In particular, you've learnt how you can use questioning to help you bring vital inner resources to bear on issues, problems and goals in a way that adds immeasurably to what you can achieve at a conscious level.

These skills all help you access the inner world that is also you, and tap into its knowledge and resources. But that inner world of you isn't just one thing: it's made up of many functions, impulses and habits; it's your physical and mental neurology; it's your past and your present; it's your different qualities and your different internal 'characters'. That's its potential richness, of course. And it can also be the source of your conflicts and some of your difficulties.

In this chapter we're going to look at some of these complexities and how you can manage them effectively. Our message is a simple one: *every* part of you has something positive to contribute to who you are and how you live your life – if you can learn to value and encourage it to play its part in the whole. And Inner Coaching can help you, by giving you a forum for fostering internal understanding and internal harmony and for exploring just how you can benefit from this amazing variety and complexity that is you.

However, valuing all of yourself and building internal relationships that work is not always easy! Have you ever been at a meeting where different points of view are all being vociferously expressed, people don't listen to each other and the Chair is ineffective? Frustrating, wasn't it? Sometimes just being yourself can feel like that, because different parts of you can each have a point of view, fail to make themselves heard, and refuse to listen to other feelings or views, with similarly disappointing or unsatisfactory results.

Have you ever had to continue working when your emotions were in turmoil? Have you ever had to refuse a fun invitation you really wanted to accept because you were so busy with work? Situations like these can make you feel a range of discomfort, from mildly uncomfortable to torn apart. We talk in everyday speech about 'a part of me' that wants this and 'another part of me' that wants that. Recognising that our selves are richly diverse, with many impulses, needs, abilities and goals, is a good starting point for examining how we can make the most of what we are and what we have.

In this chapter we're going to show you how building an alliance between the different aspects of yourself can enrich you, and how Inner Coaching can make this possible. Firstly, we're going to show you how recognising the richness of your internal make-up can be a first step towards being able to draw freely on your inner wisdom. Secondly, we're going to look at ways of managing and drawing on your varied resources so that you can act more appropriately, more wisely and more effectively.

INNER COACHING EXERCISE: DIFFERENCES AND DISCORD

► Think of a time when differences and discord didn't get to you. You could accept they existed but you were fine. Get into that state to begin to explore any internal differences and discords so you can explore in comfort.

► Spend some moments allowing yourself to wonder how it is going to help you experience the sense of valuing and being valued throughout yourself.

► It's possible that as you consider this, you may find yourself doubting your ability to value certain aspects of yourself. Allow yourself to imagine what it would be like if you could learn how they too are trying to serve your best interests.

Recognising your diversity

How many different things do you do in a day? Make breakfast, work, talk to colleagues, go out for a drink or to eat, look after your kids, shop ... Expand the time-frame to a week: perhaps you go to the gym, spend intimate time with your partner, enjoy hobbies, act as family chauffeur ... Some of these are just activities: others cluster together into the familiar patterns of expectation and behaviour that we call *roles*.

Is it the same you that is involved all these things? Yes – and no. There's the private you which includes roles like partner, friend, child, lover, parent. There may be a slightly different you involved in social activities, and another that's just you on your own, or you enjoying reading, thinking or listening to music. Yet another aspect of you may enjoy the challenges of work. Each of these roles focuses your attention and behaviour, but it also brings out a different facet of yourself, allowing you not only to behave differently but even to think and feel differently. In some of your roles you may feel confident and competent, in others quite tentative or even unconfident. Some roles may bore you, others may stimulate you. Your energy levels will vary. You are your roles – but you are also more than any of them, and indeed more than all of them put together. And Inner Coaching gives you a route to explore what each has to offer you, what you can uniquely contribute to each, and what else there may be besides ... Connecting with more of you allows you to discover a wider portfolio of possibilities, and to have more choices for the future.

INNER COACHING EXERCISE: EXPLORING ROLES

You might ask yourself the following question:

▶ How much of me is expressed through my role as X?

In asking yourself this question about a number of your key external roles, you can begin to discover which of them bring out the best in you and allow you to feel most uniquely alive. And, by contrast, there are some other related questions:

▶ Do I put up with being a certain way because I'm used to it, because I'm expected to, or because it suited me once and I've got stuck in a rut?

▶ How much of me is limited by my role as X . . . ?

▶ What important aspects of me don't currently find expression through any of my roles?

Just because you *can* be a certain way, or because you always have, doesn't mean you have to for ever more. A friend of ours was reading *Gone with the Wind*, and for a moment wished that, like the heroine Scarlett O'Hara, she could just be clasped in strong male arms and reassured. But as she told us: 'I'm not normally the kind of woman who wants that. I've trained everyone to think of me as strong and independent. My partner would never guess I might want strong arms – so if I ever do, I'll just have to ask for them!'

It's possible that using your Inner Coaching like this to explore the impact your roles have on you may involve you in deciding to make changes, for example in changing jobs or undertaking new study. Other options that come to you as a result of asking questions like these may be less apparently dramatic yet still far-reaching.

Someone we worked with thought carefully about the pattern of her life, and realised that she'd got into the habit of being kingpin in her family – as well as running her own small business. Anxious not to neglect her husband and small son, she had made sure that the house was organised and clean, that good meals were cooked, that her son was taken to school and had quality time with her at the end of the day and that she and her husband led a full social life. She tried to be a good employer to her au pair and cleaner, accommodating their availability into her crowded schedule rather than asserting her own. Suddenly she realised that there no longer seemed to be any room in her life for *her*.

So one day she sat down with herself and asked herself how she really wanted to be – and found that if she was to grow, she would have to prune the jobs she had quite drastically, even though she had willingly taken them on. When everyone was gathered together at the end of the day she told them how she felt. She said she'd thought things through and decided that if she was to be 'herself' again she would need to give up being responsible for certain things. This was the start of some major changes, which actually benefited not just her but the whole household, since the others felt more needed and more valued for the part they now played.

You and your historical selves

Roles are just one kind of way in which your diversity shows itself. There's another way which can be similarly expressive of – or similarly inappropriate to – the person you are today. We live in time, and remember our life's experiences through our senses. Memory includes not just the things we remember consciously, but a much larger body of information that's held outside of consciousness. Unconscious storage is associative, which means that like is stored with like. Holidays may be stored together – so may things to do with a foreign country you've enjoyed visiting. Fine and good – but the same process applies to sad or bad experiences. Every time you feel put down, your 'put-down' storage box gets a little fuller and its potential resonance greater, so when you feel put down again it's as though the feeling reverberates, gathering power from all the times when you felt like that before. Even if you've forgotten those incidents, they still have power to affect you here and now.

There are also other influential fragments stored away inside you: the helpless child; the playful discoverer; the rebellious teenager; the tentative young adult. Many people who have divorced in their forties or fifties have reported that when they ventured out again, hoping to make another relationship, they felt as hesitant and gauche as they had done in their early twenties. The situation triggered the historical self, with all its feelings, thoughts and behaviours.

In getting to know your historical selves, you can begin to understand much more fully what makes you respond as you do – and through your Inner Coaching you can begin to make connections within yourself so that your feelings and experiences are more available to contribute to the richness of your life. It's not appropriate to have a sulky teenager or self-absorbed six-year-old running your marriage, even temporarily, but you can really benefit from the teenager's energy and the six-year-old's ability to get absorbed in things. It's certainly not useful to have your seven-year-old self in charge of your household accounts: most seven-year-olds can't handle the complexity or the long time-frame that's required for dealing with adult finance. Your impulsive teenager probably wouldn't be much help, either. But if you're holidaying in a theme park, your seven-year-old may help you have a really good time, and if you're partying your teenager can help you enjoy dancing all night. Inner Coaching allows you to meet with them, learn from them and build relationships among them.

You need to know them well enough to be able to access what can be enabling to you now and to work with or around what's no longer appropriate or helpful. To do this is to benefit from the rich diversity that is you. If you don't, you're likely to be at the mercy of haphazard responses, so that you feel out of control or even fragmented.

You and your internal divisions

Over the last hundred years or so different psychologists have recognised human diversity and developed different models for understanding how it functions. Freud divided the mind into ego, id and superego. Gestalt offers us top-dog and under-dog. Transactional analysis works with parent, adult and child. Psychosynthesis talks of sub-personalities. It's important to understand that what these models – and there are others – offer us is not in any sense 'the truth' but rather a way of representing the complexity of human experience and tools for working with it. Psychological models relate to 'real' experience rather as a work of art does: at their best, both highlight something significant, so that you gain a new insight into what it means to be alive. As you respond to either, you make of the static model a living tool which you can work with internally. It's rather like language: dog is a word, but it doesn't bark.

Like words, the model and the work of art are representations of reality not reality itself. Mental models and works of art both draw attention to particular aspects of experience. Metaphors have a similar role: they suggest ways of thinking about something. And because your mind has the ability to work with metaphors it can use them to gain insight and make changes in your internal reality which go on to influence your external reality. Words, models and metaphors all operate symbolically.

Working with the idea that you are not one person but many doesn't mean you're falling apart. Instead, it gives you a way of recognising, exploring and working with your own diversity. In our work with individuals and groups, we find it helpful to draw upon different models to illuminate what's going on – with one important condition. We don't assume that any one part of you is inherently 'better' or 'worse' than any other part.

We assume that:

- Every part of you has potentially something to give, and to gain.

- All parts need each other.

- Every part of you has a valid origin and a valid point of view.

- Every part of you is trying in its own way to work for your benefit.

- Building an effective alliance within yourself means that you have to help all parts of you develop respect for themselves and for each other.

We've found this a useful set of assumptions for helping people, because it directs attention away from making judgements (such as good/bad, helpful/harmful) and towards exploration and discovery. Let's take an example of how this works. Perhaps you have a behaviour pattern you don't much like, or that inconveniences you in some way. How come a part of you thinks *that* behaviour could help you? Clearly the results aren't what you want – but what is the intention? Once you find the intention, you're in a position to begin looking for other, less limiting or inconvenient ways to achieve it. Assuming that all parts function best when in relation to each other, both having something to give and to gain, focuses you on helping them communicate better with each other. Paradoxically, in accepting your internal diversity you're helping your-self become more integrated.

We certainly aren't assuming that every bit of you is lovely and wonderful. Everyone has some habits or qualities they don't like that much, or that are outdated or limit them in some way. However, trying to suppress these or shut them off doesn't work: isolating them stops you connecting with them to help or influence them, and so prevents them growing or changing. When children are neglected or maltreated, they may fail to grow normally, both physically and psychologically. Ignoring or rejecting a part of yourself can have the same effect. Only when you make a connection, explore where that part originated and what it's trying to achieve for you and, above all, respect it, can you help it evolve new and more appropriate ways to contribute to the process of being you.

So what would it be like to invite two conflicting parts into a neutral space to express their different needs and wishes to you? Ask them in particular what is most important to them and what they are trying to do for you. Then consider how each needs the other to really achieve its own goal. Getting to know them like this is a great way of beginning a process of integration within you.

Connecting with your diversity

Even when you recognise in principle how diverse you are, and have maybe begun working with some of the different aspects of you that stand out in one way or another, you may wonder just how you're going to build a more complete sense of yourself and what you're capable of, or change your attitude towards some of the parts you like least. How can Inner Coaching help you do that?

INNER COACHING TIPS: THE PARTS AND THE WHOLE

The easiest way to begin is to start with what you know. You've got an overall map – called 'you'. Now you want more detail. Prepare yourself before you undertake any Inner Coaching work by setting down what you already consciously know. Make a profile of the you you're in touch with now, including aspects of yourself you like and dislike. Jot it down.

▶ Assume each part has (or had) a positive intent and find out more about it. You could use some rapid moments of inner focus to tune in to yourself and allow yourself to wonder. At the simplest, you might like to shut your eyes for a moment to cut out external distractions, and just ask yourself: *'What's that part or that behaviour trying to achieve for me?'* Respect the answer, even if it's meaning isn't immediately clear.

▶ Get to know how different parts of you each 'speak' to you. Perhaps you get a sinking feeling when asked to do something you'd rather not. Or maybe when you have to make a decision you need to wait till you have time to 'see it clearly', or 'look at it from another perspective'. Your body's own patterns of response, such as allergies or areas of weakness or susceptibility, can also sometimes act as a route for communications from your inner wisdom.

▶ The metaphors you find yourself using when you describe things, even to yourself, are letting you know what preferred signalling systems are operating. In our experience it's really valuable to pay attention to such signals – but you don't have to wait for them to come to you.

If you tend to think visually, when you're Inner Coaching ask yourself what something looks like and examine it from every angle as though you had the advantage of a computer graphics programme. You can gain even more information by extending the range of signals you tune into: if you're strongly aware of your body's responses, for example, try asking yourself what something would feel like ... or how it would sound. Even within the same sensory system there can be subtle differences. Take sound. Does that proposed holiday plan sound right to you? Does it resound like a tenor's vibrato, fall into place with a satisfying click, or does it jar? The more you practise like this, the wider the range of signals you learn to respond to. And the wider the range, the fuller the information you're able to draw on and cross-check with.

▶ It's really important, too, that you accept that this kind of personal information has validity. Respecting that the different 'languages' in which your inner wisdom can reach you are all valid because they come to you *from* you is one way in which you can benefit from the diverse information that you have inside. We've known managers in business make a successful decision that ran against logic and common sense, just because their 'nose' told them something was or wasn't quite right – only to find out much later just why their judgement was justified. The same can be true when you're managing yourself.

▶ Be on the alert for the need to update outmoded or inappropriate ways of working. Habits are the backbone of our learning and our social skills – but they can also be our straight-jackets. Just because you've always done something a certain way, or liked something, doesn't mean the habit or preference will serve you well for ever. Ask yourself how old the 'you' who's responsible is. You'll be surprised how often – and how instantly – you get a specific answer: for example, *'Eleven'* or *'Really little.'* And that may be a cue to invite that youngster in to discover their version of what's going on.

▶ Ask yourself how and in what circumstances this feeling or behaviour came about, and how it was once appropriate. Getting this kind of information puts you in a much better position to find the positive intent and generate ways to achieve it that are more appropriate to the you you are now, and the you that you want to be in future.

▶ Spend time with yourself – regularly. You can't get to know someone well without spending time with them, observing how they act and react, and finding out something about their uniqueness. The same goes for getting to know *you*. Sometimes it's good to start – or finish – the day with a few quiet minutes of special time alone with you. Or you could make use of everyday downtime like driving, washing-up, bathing or walking the dog. These kinds of undemanding activities encourage your mind to go into free flow, and if you pay attention to what's going on then you'll often find it's very informative.

▶ Another useful habit to get into is that of noticing any abrupt change of mood or state and asking yourself what caused the change, or what it might be responding to. Ask yourself: *'What was happening when (or before) I started to feel like this . . .? Did something have an impact on my state from outside – or was it something I was remembering or imagining?'* The key is connecting.

Managing your diversity

By now you'll have discovered quite a lot about the rich diversity of experiences, qualities and skills that goes to make you, you. How can you best manage all this – and what will be your guiding aims in doing so? Managing yourself can be rather like managing a complex enterprise or organisation. Think about how this can be done, and how any chosen style of management shapes the kinds of results that can be achieved.

It's the role of any CEO to have an overview and to arrange the deployment of processes and personnel in relation to an organisation's overall aims. This involves being clear about what these overall aims are. It also requires knowledge of what's involved and who is available. It involves not getting lost in the minute detail. A Chief Executive will be aware of differences of skill, approach and opinion and accept that each is valid in its own right, whether or not it should be acted upon. If you are your own chief executive, how best can you manage yourself? And how can you use your Inner Coaching to help you manage as effectively as possible, now and for the future?

The benefits of well-managed diversity

If you take care to know about the diverse sources of the wisdom within you, and attend carefully to the varied and sometimes conflicting information it's giving you, you may still have hard decisions to make, but you will at least be well-informed. You will also have access to the full range of potential information rather than blocking off parts of it. How can this be helpful to you?

- When something is complex, you won't simplify for the sake of simplifying. You will be able to work with the shades of grey.

- When you don't already have a way to deal with something, you'll be able to use Inner Coaching to consult your full range of internal 'personnel', which means you have a team working for you.

- In a time of challenge, you'll be able to change focus from frustrating detail to seeing the big picture. This will help clarify what you can do immediately.

- Inner Coaching can often help you change perspective so that you 'step outside' your immediate situation and assume an outsider's view of it: would the event seem as urgent to a Martian – or to a child playing in your neighbour's garden?

- A time of change is often one when old attitudes and patterns fail you. Reasoning only goes so far in dealing with the unknown. At such times you can take some Inner Coaching time to benefit from your inherent ability to think 'outside the box', making unusual links and unexpected syntheses.

- In a time of stagnation your familiar patterns have already failed you: you know it's not enough to go on in the same old way. You can take some Inner Coaching time to ask yourself what it is that you really, truly want. Allowing time to fantasise about how to move forward has been the beginning of change for many of our clients. Many career changes begin this way, with an initial sense of dissatisfaction, followed by a personal exploration that discovers the germ of a better idea, followed in turn by an investigation of ways and means to realise it.

Much of our thinking has been tramlined by formal education into 'convergence' – the process of narrowing options down towards a single solution. Connecting with your inherent diversity and asking yourself the vital question 'And what else …?' gives you the richer option of choice between multiple solutions.

Different approaches to self-management

Good management sees that the task is clear and that the individuals involved in working towards it are able to contribute to the best of their ability. Let's assume that your task is to be the best you can be – that is, most fully and fulfillingly you, in all the varied situations that confront you in life, and that somehow you need to organise yourself to make this possible. What skills would you need to manage the varied characters that you are? If you're going to take an active role in managing yourself, what kind of manager are you going to be?

Different metaphors suggest different styles of working with the richness that is you. Exploring them opens up a range of possibilities, and helps you to be flexible in the way you work with yourself. You can think about this as a process that happens every day, just because of the attitude you take towards the different parts of yourself when they come into play, and you can also make it a particular focus of your Inner Coaching time. There can be a place for board meetings in Inner Coaching – and for tight negotiations or mediation.

Have you ever worked in an organisation that was badly managed – where people didn't feel valued or heard, and couldn't take pride in their individual skills and contribution to the task and aims of the whole? If so, just imagine how you might be feeling inwardly if you are managing yourself in a similar way.

In the well-known stories about Thomas the Tank Engine and his friends, the Reverend W. Awdry created a character called the Fat Controller, whose job it was to tell the trains what they had to do and when. We could take the Fat Controller as one extreme type of manager. How would you feel inside if you adopted a Controller style in managing you? Sometimes you might feel relieved that 'someone else' was responsible for making decisions and 'you' only had to carry them out. But it's likely that at other times you might feel rebellious or cheeky, or want to go off and do your own thing, just as the humanised trains in those children's stories do.

By contrast, there's the *Team-leader* approach. Team-leaders certainly have to know the strengths and weaknesses of their team members to be able to get the most out of them and to utilise them well in relation to their shared task. The relationship is likely to feel more equal, and relies more on the leader's expertise and interpersonal skills than on their authority. Is this a more comfortable model for managing your diversity?

A good *Chair* makes sure that different points of view are heard, that the agenda is clear and adhered to, that decisions are made and minuted, and that follow-up tasks are allocated. The Chair is neutral, except when a casting vote is needed. Ultimately, the Chair's responsibility is to the task, and their attention is given to the process of making sure it's achieved. The Chair has the twofold authority of task and of reason. How would it feel to Chair yourself – or to be chaired by you?

Perhaps you might be happier with a *Coordinator*, or with a more performance-oriented role like *Master of Ceremonies*. Both have the responsibility for managing different skills or acts in sequence and in relation to the whole. Here the different activities, roles or 'acts' may not have much communication with each other. This may allow each to focus more clearly on their own skill, but the downside will be that they are dependent on the central organiser and that creative interplay is less likely.

Finally, how about a *Conductor*, whose job it is to synchronise the different players into a performance which is more than the sum of their collective contributions? A good conductor will bring in each instrument at the right moment, and elicit from it a kind of playing which is just right for the overall performance he is aiming for. A bad conductor may lack the ability to do this well, leaving individual players feeling unconfident and playing less well than they could.

So what kind of manager do you want to be?

Ask a favour, do a deal

Whichever kind of manager you wish to be, you will need to get cooperation from the parts of yourself you're trying to manage. Although domineering or coercive managers can sometimes get people to do things through commanding or bullying, usually there's a payback at some point. Maybe it's in the form of minimal compliance; maybe there's active sabotage; maybe there's a sullen resistance. Most of us have felt all of these responses at some time when someone asked us 'the wrong way'. But when it's you asking you, you don't have the luxury of going home and complaining! Willing cooperation becomes vital.

So how do you get it? In our experience, managers of every kind get further if they:

- Are clear about what it is they want

- Specify what it is they are asking the other party to do

- Take on board any reservations the other person has and try to accommodate them if possible

- Find ways in which the desired behaviour can be advantageous to the person being asked

- Are respectful in their approach

- Where possible, offer some form of reward – even if it's just 'Thank you'.

INNER COACHING TIPS: MAKING DEALS

Think of asking a favour as seeking to do a deal. Deals have to have some benefit for all parties. And Inner Coaching gives you the perfect means, and the most supportive space, for doing this. Here's how this can work:

▶ If you want your body to marshal its energies for a specially taxing occasion, or your mind to come up with some really creative ideas, or to be courageous in a situation you know you're going to find threatening – what do you have to offer in return? Promising – and then giving – yourself some time off, taking time to relish your new ideas, actually celebrating your achievement, all these are simple ways of returning the favour to yourself.

▶ You could use some inner time to collect ideas for rewards and treats you can offer yourself. Some friends of ours then write their ideas down and collect them in a bowl: on a day when one or other deserves a reward or a break, they pull out one of the ideas and just do it.

▶ If your body has worked hard at keeping your energy going so that you can enjoy a party, or complete a difficult task to a deadline, what it really needs is downtime. An early night, restful activities, a lie-in, perhaps a day off or even a short break are what's needed. Will you keep your side of the bargain?

▶ If your mind has been really stretched, find ways to celebrate and enjoy what it has created. Seek respite in different activities.

This is how you show yourself respect and create balance in your life. If you don't do this you use up your credit and goodwill and the result is declining cooperation from within. If you take yourself for granted the rest of you will be less willing to make the effort next time.

Managing your impulses

We've talked a lot about valuing and encouraging the diversity within you. And we've shown you how you can create and make a neutral and welcoming space in your Inner Coaching which will facilitate this and help with negotiation and even conflict resolution. However, once you have established communication with the different parts of you, how are you going to know which to and follow, and whose side to take when they don't agree? How do you know when you're being railroaded by impulse? How do you distinguish between being impulsive and being spontaneous – in other words, how can you tell when an impulse really is worth acting on?

There's one vital test you can make when you're wondering whether to act on these messages from your inner world: we think of it as checking your personal ecology. It's our experience that when something *is* right it feels right, looks right, sounds right, smells right and tastes right. It just fits with every bit of you. There's a sense of 'of course' about it. You may feel yourself relaxing, or it may be as if things have just 'fallen into place'. That's the litmus test. Sometimes it's so clear there's no danger of you *not* getting the message – but it's good to make a habit of checking in with yourself *every* time, either by learning to monitor more rapidly and more sensitively or by taking specific Inner Coaching time for checking things out, because sometimes the signals are less obvious.

When you're being railroaded by an impulse the desire may seem strong, but if you really pay attention you'll be able to pick up some unease somewhere. You're quite likely to find yourself trying to justify the action you propose taking, bolstering it up with persuasive arguments and reasons. And once you've followed your impulse and done what it demanded, you'll be seeking even more reasons retrospectively. If questioned, you are likely to feel defensive. This isn't necessarily because the action was the wrong one. Rather, it's because you weren't fully in agreement with yourself about it. And you may even find yourself putting off the inner checking process we're talking about – just because the part of you that's railroading you doesn't want to allow the opposition a voice! Finding yourself putting off such ecological checks is usually a sign that you really need to do them.

INNER COACHING EXERCISE: CHECK YOUR ECOLOGY

▶ Take a moment now to test this out by remembering some recent decisions you've made. Were they spontaneous, feeling right inside, or were they driven by impulse without internal consultation and agreement?

▶ Do you have your own litmus tests in addition to the sense of rightness we've described? The more aware you become of these small but significant inner responses the more finely tuned your responses can be.

The art of building alliances

One way to summarise what we've been discussing throughout this chapter is that it's aimed at helping you build a working alliance amongst the different parts of yourself. Allies are rarely in complete agreement with each other, but they do have significant areas of overlap in their values and their goals. The art of building alliances is to help each party to the alliance focus on what it has in common, so that its policy and actions relate to that and to what each will gain from the support of the other. Though there can be many successful variations on how you can use your Inner Coaching to facilitate this process, the core steps are these:

1. Seek out, respect and trust all information in all sensory systems equally.

2. Find out the positive intent of each part involved.

3. Discover what values are involved, and help your internal allies build a sense of their shared values.

4. Cultivate mutual respect among them.

5. Seek for a working agreement – and be prepared to monitor its effects and adjust it if necessary.

From the centredness of your neutral and welcoming space you can achieve all these things. You can talk to the different parts of yourself, allow them to have their say – and ask them to tell you and each other what values and intentions are involved. You can listen attentively. You can employ words and phrases – and above all, questions, tactfully and supportively. You can draw on all your best interpersonal skills – and use them internally.

If at first this feels strange, keep going. Remind yourself that we all have partial, often unrecognised, conversations with ourselves. You are going to take this one step further, make it more inclusive and more effective. And doing so is going to help you build an internal alliance that is richly diverse, resourceful and productive beyond your expectations.

> *What is synergy? Simply defined, it means that the whole is greater than the sum of its parts. It means that the relationship which the parts have to each other is a part in itself. It is not only a part, but the most catalytic, the most empowering, the most unifying, and the most exciting part.*
>
> Stephen R. Covey, *The 7 Habits of Highly Effective People*

Chapter Ten

Discovering Your Purpose, Vision and Spirit

I nner Coaching has many immediate and practical applications, from the nuts and bolts of everyday living to the solving of major puzzles and problems. Now we want to show you how it can also help you answer some of the most important questions in life: *'What do I want?'* *'What am I here for?'* and *'How does my life fit into the greater scheme of things?'*

These questions take us beyond immediate everyday experiences, and draw attention to three things that can give life a more profound and satisfying meaning – your purpose, vision and spirit. In this chapter we're going to show you how Inner Coaching can help you explore and enhance these dimensions of your life.

As human beings, once our baseline survival needs – food, shelter, reproduction – have been met, we seem programmed to want more. We look to enhancing our experience of life and transcending our limitations. Indeed, this may be the defining difference between human beings and all other known species. In addition to pleasure, we look for purpose, we aim for self-realisation or self-actualisation, and we search and hope for meaning. We seek to discover more about ourselves, each other and the world around us. We are driven by a developing sense of commitment to personal and social ethics to create better possibilities and to right wrongs.

These are the themes that underlie many myths and legends: Homer's *Odyssey*, the stories of the Old and New Testaments, Beowulf's vengeance on the monster Grendel, the legends of King Arthur and the search for the Grail. *The Lord of the Rings* and *Star Wars*, are contemporary additions to the genre. Seeking a significant quest is important to us all because it involves the search for meaning and the hope of discovery. And whether the goal is external, as in the search for treasure or lost civilisations, or internal, as in spiritual exploration, it involves us on many levels.

So far in this book, we have shown you some of the ways in which, through Inner Coaching, you can connect with your unconscious mind-body wisdom and draw upon it to enhance your everyday resourcefulness. If you've been doing the Inner Coaching exercises you'll have begun to discover something of *what* you can do, and some suggestions for *how* you can do it. This chapter is about the *why* of it all.

So let's begin with, '*Why bother?*' The reason for actively engaging with yourself through Inner Coaching is that, in our experience, it enriches your life and gives you access to a wealth of resources for living it better. When we teach people Inner Coaching, they so often say, 'I wish I'd learnt this before now.' They have a way of being in touch with themselves and of accessing their inner wisdom. And it's such a relief to have a reliable and easy way to make that connection. But then, even more possibilities begin to open up.

Think of learning a foreign language. At first, your aim may be to identify everyday things and ask for them: items in shops and cafes, directions, normal exchanges of greeting and farewell. Then it's good to be able to comment on the weather, ask simple questions and make the tentative beginnings of conversation. But there comes a time when you want to be able to have a real conversation in which you exchange ideas, reflect, explore and speculate. This is the stage we're getting to with Inner Coaching – how you can use it to help you with the biggest questions of all.

Like physical muscles, the skills of Inner Coaching develop as they are used. We hope that already you'll have begun to notice some of the enrichment they can bring. Using them to seek out your own individual purpose, vision and spirit can make your life truly worth living.

> '*Hallo!*' said Piglet, '*what are* you *doing?*'
> '*Hunting,*' said Pooh.
> '*Hunting what?*'
> '*Tracking something,*' said Winnie-the-Pooh very mysteriously.

> 'Tracking what?' said Piglet, coming closer.
> 'That's just what I ask myself. I ask myself, What?'
> 'What do you think you'll answer?'
> 'I shall have to wait until I catch up with it,' said Winnie-the-Pooh.

A.A. Milne, *Winnie-the-Pooh*

Often we are like Pooh, feeling impelled to search without quite knowing what we're searching for. But we certainly know when we've found it! Think back to a time when you were not sure what to do next. Maybe you were faced with a decision about a career, or a relationship. Maybe you were experiencing some kind of crisis of belief or faith. When you eventually made that decision or reached a point of clarification, how did you know? In our experience, most people have a strong kinaesthetic sense of rightness or fitness. It's as though their whole being 'just knows'.

Equally, a sense of things *not* being right may arrive long before the conscious mind catches up with just why a decision that seemed logical isn't wholly right after all. And where someone's life seems to lack these essential qualities of meaning and purpose, they will know that too. Without meaning, people feel lethargic, irritable or unfocused. Once we are beyond the basic need to survive, it seems that meaning is as essential to us as the air we breathe.

A friend of ours had this instinctive sense that something was missing in her life. She was feeling concerned because her freelance work projects seemed to be tapering off or were being blocked. She realised she was missing the stimulus that they gave her, but didn't know what she needed to do next. By contrast, she had just had a really exciting day working to raise money for charity by competing at some on-the-edge physical challenges, including tank driving and rock climbing. This day had tested her existing skills and developed them even further – and it had given her a great buzz. What she had taken on for charity became a source of great personal enrichment. As she talked about it, she realised that she needed a similar sense of challenge, meaning and buzz in her professional life. That's what was missing. This didn't mean that, even using Inner Coaching, she could find 'the answer' all at once. But it did mean that she knew what she was looking for – and that she had the tools to go about finding it.

We'd go so far as to say that without some access to your inner dimension, you really can't get the most from life. Even if you think you don't want much, just because you're a human being you'll always have some kind of instinctive need for stretch, buzz and meaning. Deep down, we all seem to really need these things. However, you can only go so far if you confine yourself to going for them just in the outer world. To get the most and find them inwardly, you'll need to engage with your own inner dimensions – and that's where Inner Coaching comes in.

Everything you've been learning so far will make the search easier. In addition, expanding your theatre of operations by engaging with your other-than-conscious mind will accelerate the whole process. People we've worked with have sometimes said that the shock and discovery of learning to engage with this part of themselves is like suddenly discovering they have limbs they've never used before – basic human equipment that can make life both simpler and richer.

We've identified three aspects of this search. We think of them as a hierarchy or pyramid, in which each higher level includes and goes beyond the levels below. In ascending order, they are: purpose, vision and spirit. We're going to look at each in turn and see how Inner Coaching can help you discover them and make them come alive.

Purpose

To have a purpose is to have a sense of direction. Purpose can be simple and unambitious, and it can also be grand, when it's directed towards achieving a greater vision. Purpose on its own is getting from A to B, whether it's just along the road, sitting a series of exams to qualify for a career, buying a house or developing a friendship. Having purpose means you know where you want to go. There are often times when you may be unsure, are at a point of transition where an old purpose seems insufficient and a new one has not emerged, or where you are having to make a choice.

Often purpose can be formed, encouraged or even dictated by outside people or forces. Ian remembers a client who came for help, saying: 'I'm a dentist. My mother wanted me to be a dentist. I've always been a dentist. Now I've a house and mortgage, a wife and family, a secretary and an assistant and a rented building to pay for. I never wanted to be a dentist, but now I'll have to go on being a dentist for ever.' He had a purpose, but it did not feel like his own. We would say that he did have a purpose – running a practice and supporting his family – but he did not have a vision for his life. Inner Coaching helped him develop a vision, *his* vision. It had a lot to do with caring for people – and not much to do with dentistry. Over the next few years he turned his life around and made it *his* life.

Even when we are clear that our purpose is of our choosing, working towards it can sometimes still be joyless. 'Going through the hoops' on the way to a qualification or doing without treats in order to save for something both have a valid purpose: you may be committed to the goals involved and willing to do what's needed to achieve them, yet at the same time feel uninspired. Your purpose has given you direction, taken your time and your energy, but given little back along the way. It's possible that even once you've achieved the goal you've been working towards, your feeling of satisfaction may not last all that long, because once you've achieved your goal, you just shift the goalposts and don't get to enjoy it. You get the qualification, which means that you can get a new job, perhaps more money and so on. You bought the bigger house, moved to a nice neighbourhood, have more space to move around in, can acquire more possessions and so on. But these changes may not address any of your deeper needs and desires.

Purpose is valuable: it can be the drive that gets you improving your life or sorting out your difficulties. We have known plenty of purposeful people whose main drive was to get away from poverty, ignorance or unhappiness. This 'away from' drive has one drawback, though – it's defined by what you *don't* want. Anywhere that's better will do. Problem-solving is a great way to feel purposeful, but the more it occupies your thoughts and your time the less able you are to take a longer view. We've known people who would have felt quite lost if they'd ever come to the end of their problem list, because they simply hadn't learnt how to work out what they really wanted. They hadn't learnt the skill.

Having a sense of purpose is rewarding and often pleasurable, and affects your sense of self. It will certainly involve the expenditure of energy, and this can be energising or enervating. Our friend's individuality was confirmed by her voluntary work, and she felt re-energised because meeting the challenges revealed to her more about herself and what her capabilities were. But until the dentist looked beyond the immediate purposes of maintaining a practice and a standard of living to seek a meaningful vision, his individuality remained *un*confirmed, even partially negated, and he felt drained. Where you truly own a goal, and work purposefully towards it, you will have a sense of personal engagement that in some sense confirms your individuality.

INNER COACHING TIPS: WHAT'S THE PURPOSE?

▶ Take an activity that absorbs you. Ask yourself: *'What purpose does this serve for me?'*

▶ Take the answer you get, and use the laddering method to repeat the same question after each answer you get until you know there is no further to go, so that each time your answers enlarge, from small, perhaps immediate, purposes to greater ones.

▶ Take this past week. Think of the activities you've been engaged in. Ask yourself: *'What purpose drove them?'* Is this a purpose you want to own?

▶ Then ask yourself: *'How might this purpose be enlarged to become a purpose I'd be proud to have for my life?'*

▶ Then consider: *'Could this, perhaps, be enlarged to become part of my personal vision?'*

Purpose is a valuable and worthwhile thing to have. It brings meaning and achievement to what you do. It will call on, and may help you develop, your knowledge and skills. It gives or confirms your sense of direction, and allows you to keep on track and measure your progress. It helps you prioritise how you spend your energy, time and money in relation to what you seek, and can help make each day meaningful and worthwhile. But there is more to life. Ian sometimes calls it 'purpose plus'. That's when purpose becomes part of a vision.

Vision

What is vision? In this context it's a pole star, a guiding light, that illuminates and guides your life. It informs and directs your immediate purposes, relating them to something bigger and more meaningful. It gives you a mission. It adds deep satisfaction to purpose, passion to energy, uniqueness to individuality. Vision means you know what you want or need to do and why it is important. Vision helps you align what you're doing with your beliefs and your values. So your commitment is greater, your involvement in the process of getting to your goal is deepened, and your satisfaction in achieving even small steps towards it is enhanced.

Having a vision means that you have a really clear idea of where you are going – one that adds the why to the what and the how. For some people, vision will be literally that, an internal image of how things will look in the future. But being able to imagine something in visual detail is not the same as having a vision. A vision gives you a rationale and a direction. It's a guide, not just an end to aim at. You can live it as you go.

You may never fully achieve your vision – in fact, vision almost always goes beyond what is actually doable. That's really the point. If you already knew how to do what's involved and already had the skills, it would be more like living life with purpose. Having a vision is a way of stretching yourself and reminding yourself that there is yet more. It's a way of living according to a dream.

This kind of dreaming can be scary. It has you at the edge of your possibilities. And that's just why daring to dream can be enlarging and enlivening. So how can you begin to enlarge your sense of yourself and your life, and discover your vision?

Well, do you know what your vision is now? If not, what would it be like to have one? How would it make a difference to your life – now and in the future? Who are the people you see as having vision? How would you say it affects the way they live?

INNER COACHING EXERCISE: VISION QUEST

▶ Take yourself into your welcoming Inner Coaching place, outside the pressures of the here and now – and let yourself dare to dream.

▶ Consider yourself and your everyday life. Become an observer for a while. Notice what currently gives you a sense of purpose, whether it's large or small, personal or professional, external or internal. Then pull back from the detail so that you become aware of the broader context of meanings and values.

> ▶ Do your immediate purposes relate to a wider vision – or might they come to? What would have to happen to make your dream – your vision – a reality?

For some people, like our dentist, this kind of exercise enables them to discover just what needs to be cleared out of the way so that their vision can become clearer and they can make it live more fully in their lives. Practicalities and immediate purposes can serve a vision, or clutter its path and make it harder to follow. Sometimes, it's a matter of fine-tuning rather than making huge changes.

Often, the hopes and ambitions we had as children and young adults spring from a profound if unarticulated sense of just who we could be, given the opportunity. And often, these 'wannabes' get left behind – or perhaps are even dismissed as 'unrealistic'. Perhaps they are – in the literal sense of how we thought of them then. But what was the vision underlying them?

▶ Think about what you dreamt of becoming when you were little. Take some time to reconnect with the vision your dream represented. Think about what you dreamt of becoming when you were not so little. Have you lost sight of these? Have these changed? Could these still enlarge and enliven your life in some way?

Spirit

To purpose and vision, spirit adds so much more. To your pleasure and buzz it adds joy; to your energy and passion it adds playfulness, and to your individuality and uniqueness it adds wholeness and a sense of harmony. It also informs every level of your activity and being with a consistent meaning.

So what is this spiritual dimension, and where does it come from? In our everyday language there are pointers to what it may be, and to what it isn't. We talk of the 'life of the spirit', a life which may be nurtured through formal religion, personal spiritual practice or through profound experiences such as playing or listening to music, meditating, responding to beauty in nature or feeling you are part of something larger. We also think of the spirit as the individual supreme essence of a living creature: that which is present throughout its life and which, according to differing views of death, may then either be transformed or depart entirely.

Within the Christian religion, there is a special place for spirit referred to in Latin as the Spiritus Sanctus or Holy Spirit. But we also talk of someone giving a spirited performance, of high-spirited behaviour. We talk of people and horses who are 'spirited', meaning that they are lively, perhaps even wilful at times.

You can feel a sense of this in yourself, or in others, in many different contexts. Think of a horse and rider jumping a huge fence or performing intricate movements. The very best appear united as one creature: the immense power of the horse is truly and willingly at the rider's disposal, yet there's no dominance involved. The performance is almost playful, apparently lighthearted for all the extreme of effort involved. It's truly 'spirited'. In *The Ethics and Passion of Dressage*, the great equestrian teacher Charles de Kunffy says:

> For the horse and rider to appear as merged in the effort of motion such as with the image of the Centaur ... The rider must offer his mind to guide the body of the horse, while both of their spirits are animated by the joy of this partnership ... A partnership born of spirited love.

It's our experience that just by being human, you too have within you the potential for such effortlessness of being. It's not about what you do: it's about the way that you do it.

Sometimes, people report that they feel like this when they connect with their innermost selves during Inner Coaching – not every time, but often enough to surprise them. At these times you can have a sense of being at one with yourself, of being aligned in everything you feel and think, in the big things and the small things, which is instantly recognisable and truly spiritual. These are some of the 'peak experiences' of life – those moments of heightened awareness and fulfilment which seem to epitomise all that's best about being alive.

The dimension of spirit is one which allows you to connect with others and even with the universe, to have a sense of your individual, unique part in your culture, your civilisation – and beyond that in the wider history of mankind. In this way, it offers you both an external and internal point of reference, helping you to make sense of your experience, to evaluate it, and to know when you need to seek further. It's your integrity – not just in the limited sense of 'being true to yourself' but in the larger sense of you 'being wholly yourself'.

INNER COACHING EXERCISE: AMONG THE PEAKS

▶ Allow yourself to enter a mindful state, and to recollect a moment of heightened intensity that was for you a peak experience.

▶ Consider how it might exemplify the purpose, vision and spirit in your life.

▶ Do this for three different episodes in your life.

▶ Ask yourself what common threads emerge.

We know that many people have found a new sense of purpose, a greater and more dynamic vision, and beyond that an awareness of the spiritual dimension of their life, with the help of their own Inner Coaching. We would argue that these things are as much part of your personal inheritance as your in-built disposition to growth and to health. Like growth and like health, they can be thwarted. But in the same way that most of us can wake up in the morning and know 'instinctively' when we are off-colour, so your internal wisdom can let you know when you're 'off-colour' in terms of your purpose, your vision and your spirit.

INNER COACHING EXERCISE: UNIQUENESS OF SPIRIT

▶ Allow yourself to enter your Inner Coaching state, and imagine being to become open to the whole of yourself and your experience. You might have a sense of reaching out, of welcoming in, of allowing, or of being quietly and profoundly receptive. Visually you might notice particular colours and panoramas. If words work for you, ask yourself, *'What helps me to be more in touch with my uniqueness of spirit?'* Then expand your enquiry and ask, *'What helps me to be in touch with the spirit in others and in the world?'* Be gently curious. Allow your mind to take its own direction and make its own connections.

Many people ignore or have blunted their awareness of the spirit in themselves. Some even find it difficult or threatening to be receptive in this way. Probably all of us blunt ourselves from time to time to such messages. We haven't time. We can't stop. The boss expects. Turning a blind eye like this for any length of time can mean that our internal signals about purpose, vision and spirit have to get louder and louder. If we ignore them we experience ever greater unease which can culminate in 'dis-ease'. That's a signal most people are trained to recognise when it gets loud enough. Then you take action, but will you address the real issue?

When you lack purpose, vision or spirit in your life you lack something as essential to your inner being as food and drink is to your body. Instead of waiting till you're starving and dying of thirst we would like you to be able to know what can nourish you right now.

If you pay attention to your own experience you can know immediately when and why you are well, happy, excited, fulfilled, creative or spiritually alive. Only then can you do more of what works. Making a habit of Inner Coaching gives you a great way to monitor yourself – and the opportunity to make small adjustments rather than having to wait until big ones are needed.

INNER COACHING EXERCISE: EXPLORING PURPOSE, VISION AND SPIRIT

▶ What gives me pleasure and energy, and enhances my sense of individuality?

▶ When do I have a sense of purpose, of vision and spirit in my life? When have I felt this in the past?

▶ What lets me know when I'm out of touch with these important elements in myself and my life – and what tells me when I'm connected with them?

The nature of the evidence

We've asked you to pay attention to the feelings that tell you about the presence or absence of purpose, vision and spirit because it's our experience that feelings, especially physical or kinaesthetic ones, are the most natural and frequent source of information we have. What tells you that your life is lacking in purpose, or on the other hand that you're on track for your personal Everest of exploration or challenge, is usually a kinaesthetic change: it may be a frisson, a release of energy, a sense of excitement, a feeling of engagement with an idea or a possibility. You can't have a feeling or a thought without it being in some way reflected in your physiology. Following the feelings leads you to the information. Building information like this helps you become more aware of what purpose, vision and spirit mean for you. You can refine your questioning further by asking yourself:

▶ Are any particular activities, goals or aims involved ?

▶ Are there any reliable triggers?

▶ Are there any recurring patterns of external circumstances which generally tend to make me feel this way?

▶ Are there any kinds of people who help me feel like this?

▶ Do I behave in any special ways at these times?

As you ask yourself these questions, you may be surprised by the amount of information you have. Until you pay yourself this kind of detailed attention, you will not know how much information you do have – and the extent of the wisdom within you.

Once you know the elements that make up these qualities as far as you are concerned, you can seek them out to enhance and refresh your purpose, vision and spirit. You can replicate what works, and have it again. But you can go further by asking yourself that great coaching question: *'And what else?'* Because so often, when you ask yourself this in Inner Coaching, there *will* be something else, which can add even more.

Chapter Eleven

Your Exotic Gifts

nner Coaching can help you make the most of gifts from your unconscious intelligence in two ways: first, it can help you recognise and accept them when they arrive unasked for; and secondly, it can help you actively seek them out.

In this chapter and the next we want to show you how Inner Coaching can help you become more receptive to these gifts, and more able to value and work with them. In this chapter we're going to consider gifts which can easily be mistrusted because they seem more exotic; and in Chapter 12 we're going to take a closer look at those of your gifts which are 'everyday', and therefore more easily overlooked or taken for granted.

The word 'gift' is interesting in itself, because it has two important meanings – both of which apply here. It denotes 'a thing given or received', and it has also come to mean 'a natural ability or talent'. Inner Coaching both helps you receive the first kind of gift and develop the second. It's able to do this because it is a means of building a more open relationship with all of yourself, it allows you to become more sensitive and receptive to what this relationship can potentially deliver – and as you become more relaxed and more fluent in using the process, it becomes a gift in itself.

Unconscious intelligence is a proven fact. The need to wait for inspiration rather than to manufacture it – to envisage the conscious self as the

> recipient of gifts from a workplace to which consciousness has no access
> – is likewise undeniable. We need a new conception of the unconscious –
> one which gives it back its intelligence, and which reinstalls it within the
> sense of self – if we are to regain the ways of knowing with which it is
> associated.
>
> Guy Claxton, *Hare Brain, Tortoise Mind*

As you make Inner Coaching a regular part of your life, you are accepting this unconscious workplace as valid, and giving yourself permission to get involved with it. You are engaging in a process which has a life of its own. In our experience, you're entering into a cycle of events, reactions, responses and further events which you will find self- and life-enhancing. By contrast, when you deny or block this process, you're entering into another cycle, which is ever more limited and self-alienating. The first is a *virtuous* cycle, the second a *vicious* one. (See diagrams opposite)

The nature of cycles, of course, is that they can go on repeating themselves. There's a widespread recognition that vicious cycles exist, but much less awareness that virtuous ones do, and that they can play just as significant a part in shaping your life.

The gifts of your inner world are there for your taking, and Inner Coaching is one important means by which you can elicit and receive them. However, some of these gifts come in packages which can be difficult to decipher. Among them are 'gut feelings', intuition, and mind-body miracles and dreams, the subjects of this chapter.

Most of us have learnt to be wary of what can't be demonstrated and so 'proved' to the conscious part of the mind. If you rely largely or solely on what *can* be proved, you might end up thinking of the workings of the less accessible parts of your mind as odd, unreliable or even phoney. Get into this kind of thinking and you close down so much that could enrich and benefit you.

We find it more useful to start from the assumption that anything that comes from the other-than-conscious part of the mind is (1) genuine and (2) potentially useful. This focuses your attention on how you can work out what meaning to attribute to these signals from your inner world, and what potential value they may have for you. In our experience it makes sense to assume that there *is* meaning, and that it is often quite idiosyncratic. But how you get at it will need to be different. It's clear from dreams and from creative activities (ranging from the arts

Here's how each works.

Virtuous cycle

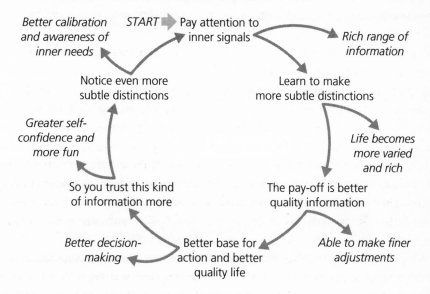

Vicious cycle

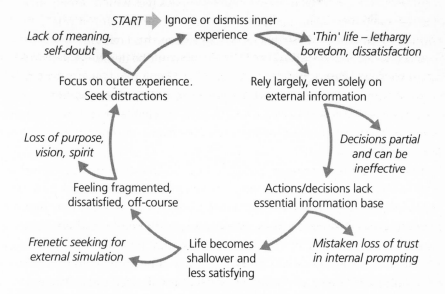

to making puns) that our minds work associatively. Associative thinking is different from the logic favoured by your conscious mind. The only obstacle to taking these kind of thought processes seriously is that they are far less easy for the conscious mind to understand.

As a traveller in a strange land, would you rather be the kind that's welcomed because you are respectful, curious and willing to learn how things are done there, or one that's hated because you insist on trying to impose your country's customs everywhere because they are 'better' or 'more enlightened'? If you travel with interest, wonder and humility, you're much more likely to be enriched. And the same is true when you journey within.

Every time you watch a movie, read a novel or see a play, you're demonstrating that you already know how to do this. Samuel Taylor Coleridge described the process as 'That willing suspension of disbelief for the moment, which constitutes poetic faith.' You know film sets aren't 'real'. You know a play is quite literally staged. But you suspend your disbelief to be able to really enjoy what's on offer. Anyone who stood up in the middle of a performance and started protesting that it wasn't real would be regarded as just missing the point. They don't understand the dramatic conventions or the rules of the game. But this is exactly what people often do in relation to the creative process of their own inner world.

Instead, how would it be to approach your gut feelings, your intuition, your amazing capacity to heal and your dream life with this willing suspension of disbelief? Then you could step over the threshold of everyday thinking into a new world of understanding – and a new world of possibilities. Because when you engage with your inner workplace, it can deliver results that are actual and even measurable in your external experience.

Gut feelings

Let's start with those tantalising signals from within, your gut feelings.

Everybody has gut feelings, but knowing whether – and when – to trust them can be an issue for many people. In fact, the miracle is not that we have them but that so often we manage to edit them out. Now that we know about the subtle interconnectedness within the body-mind, we can begin to realise that *any* change, *anywhere* within the totality of the body-mind, has the potential to communicate more or less influentially with any or every other part. So when you receive and process information in one area, processing it will send ripples into other areas.

The difficulty for the conscious mind is that when that processing is happening unconsciously, and the effects 'arrive' in your awareness in the form of a gut feeling, they don't come with decoding instructions or supporting evidence. And another problem is that this happens so fast. Your unconscious body-mind processes complex information much faster than your conscious mind ever could, so it can reach its own conclusions about something outside of your awareness before you've had time to evaluate it rationally. A positive conclusion will be translated in microseconds into positive physical sensations; a negative one into anger, sadness or even pain; and a confused one into a sense of unease or discomfort.

One way to help yourself be more receptive to such kinaesthetic communication is to learn to acknowledge that these instant sensations are a kind of personal shorthand, and to add the message to any information you have at a conscious level. That way, you get a more rounded impression. Sometimes you'll get that conscious information much later. We have all encountered people who had a gut feeling they shouldn't trust someone or do something, yet went ahead because they couldn't find a reason, and later regretted it. Equally, plenty of people have successfully 'backed a hunch' in their personal or working lives and been lastingly grateful they went beyond the available evidence and trusted to their instincts.

SPECIAL EXERCISE: EVIDENCE GATHERING FOR YOUR CONSCIOUS MIND

▶ Begin to collect and document your own gut feelings. That means paying attention to them. You might like to keep a notebook so you can track them. You could begin by writing down significant gut feelings you've had in the past. Did they turn out to be informative? Have you subsequently found out just why you felt as you did? Were you able to use them to help you avoid unpleasant or damaging experiences or to manage and enrich your life?

> ▶ Conscious review and documentation like this can help your conscious mind collect the kind of 'evidence' it feels familiar with, encouraging it to become more accepting and pay more attention in future.

INNER COACHING EXERCISE: REVIEWING GUT FEELINGS

> ▶ Take a gut feeling you once had, which you dismissed or didn't act on. Allow yourself to review it in your mindful state, and begin to wonder what may have given rise to it. Invite your unconscious to help you explore just how its message came to take that particular form.
>
> ▶ Ask within for help in recognising your gut feelings more readily.

Intuition

We suggest that what we often label intuition is actually a judgement based on 'weak signals' which you pick up unconsciously – that is to say, without conscious awareness being alerted. In *Hare Brain, Tortoise Mind* Guy Claxton argues that we can sharpen our ability to 'make use of the mass of weak impressions that underlie – and are usually neglected by – our normal ways of seeing and knowing. It is possible to increase one's *conscious* sensitivity to what had previously been going on at an unconscious level'.

The concept of weak signals is a really helpful one. One of the characteristics of effective leaders in business and politics is that they notice and respond to information before others do: they pick up faint trends, notice small and subtle shifts and are prepared to act on them. This gives them the edge and helps them stay 'ahead of the game'. This is our virtuous cycle in action.

The point is that the information is actually there: when your intuition tells you something, it's because you have been unconsciously monitoring and registering differences like these. The better you get at doing this, and the more able you are to trust the information received this way, the more you have to work with. You still have to consider its significance and how best to act on it, but you have more information to act on and you may be able to do so faster.

This can be helpful in different spheres of your life. The intuition that a business deal – or a friendship – is turning sour, or about to take off; the intuition that something or someone isn't to be trusted; the sense that you're sickening for something long before you actually feel ill; all these can be helpful advance signals based on weak information. Acting rapidly may save you from the impact of 'stronger' signals!

INNER COACHING EXERCISE: EXAMINING INTUITION

▶ Take some time to reflect on examples of your own intuition. What weak signals were you picking up?

▶ Did you find it easy or difficult to take yourself seriously and to act on what you 'knew'?

▶ Next time you sense something intuitively, take some Inner Coaching time to explore the message in this way, so that you can benefit more fully from it.

Mind-body communication

One of the most exciting aspects of Inner Coaching is that you can actively use it to monitor, maintain and restore your own mind-body health. And this gives you much greater potential influence.

There are plenty of extreme examples of mind-body work. Miraculous 'cures' from life-threatening illnesses and astounding recoveries from major accidents are well documented. And like the other exotic gifts we've been talking about, they can have a foundation in solid 'fact'. The word miracle comes from the Latin *miraculum,* which in itself gives us a clue: it means 'an object of wonder'. When we hear about just what is possible, or experience influencing our own health, we have the opportunity to reconsider our beliefs about possibility and impossibility. And as we do, the realm of what is possible for us as individuals often expands. Our experience suggests that each and every one of us has the potential to have more influence on the totality of our well-being than we may realise – and that's where Inner Coaching comes in.

Once you accept that mind and body consist of interrelated systems, and that chemical and electrical messengers constantly convey complex information back and forth at many levels, it becomes easier to understand how few health outcomes can be predicted reliably, whether for good or ill. Ernest Rossi gives some notable examples and documents the scientific research that begins to explain them in his book *The Psychobiology of Mind-Body Healing*; and Deepak Chopra has explored the almost infinitesimal molecular basis upon which beliefs and emotions may be 'converted' into illness and health in *Quantum Healing*. A different way to think of mind-body miracles is that they draw our attention to *the edges of what we believed was possible*, and invite us to push back the boundaries of how we think about ourselves. Here are some examples.

Christopher Reeve, the actor best known for playing Superman, became a paraplegic after breaking his neck in a riding accident. He had no sensation or motor control below the neck, and the prognosis was that he never would have. The medical profession, in fact, expected him to die. But he was determined to recover and eventually to walk again, and he was fortunate enough to be able to fund 24-hour care.

It was his own inner resources which made the difference. He got his assistants to give him three or four hours of daily help in exercising his body to keep his systems functioning and to prevent muscle wastage. After seven years without apparent improvement, he found one day that he could move one finger just a little, even though recovery from this particular injury was previously unknown and his doctors believed it to be impossible. This was the beginning of a slow and continuing increase in further movement. Reeve said that since his accident he had never once dreamt of himself in a wheelchair. For him, this reflected his firm belief that one day he would walk again.

The great hypnotherapist Milton Erickson contracted polio at the age of 17, becoming totally paralysed, apart from his eyelids. He was outraged one night to overhear the doctors telling his mother that he would not be alive in the morning, and was determined to survive. During a lengthy period of immobility, he thought intensely about all the activities he had enjoyed before his illness, and relived them in great detail in his mind. He also spent hours watching his baby sister as she learnt to walk, imagining how it must feel to make those experimental movements and progress towards mastery and control. He too began to find himself making small movements as he imagined them so intensely in his mind. In this way a remarkable self-recovery began, which resulted in Erickson walking again.

How can you take advantage of your own miraculous interconnectedness and benefit from Inner Coaching to maintain or restore your health? People who have made remarkable recoveries seem to have certain things in common. They use medical information as a basis for action – *but it is of their choosing*. They're not in denial – it's just that they don't go along with the official prognosis. They invariably go within and develop their own treatment plan based on what makes sense to them – while at the same time working with medics and caregivers. They are also prepared to put in hours of intense and demanding work, both physically and mentally. They are committed and take the time to imagine a better, different future for themselves.

Commitment and imagination are at the heart of the process. The body does indeed have an amazing ability to defend and repair itself. You can help it in this work by using Inner Coaching to give yourself the time and energy to encourage this.

Inner Coaching and mind-body work

There are a number of routes you can follow, and we suggest that you experiment to find what works best for you.

Establishing a baseline awareness of your well-being

▶ Rather than waiting until you feel off-colour, use some Inner Coaching time to tune in and monitor how you are. What's it like to feel comfortable, at ease and well in yourself?

▶ Check in with yourself regularly in this way, until you come to know very rapidly how you are doing. Then make it a regular part of you self-maintenance, perhaps by tacking on a rapid self-check when you are doing other daily routines like showering or cleaning your teeth. Make it automatic.

▶ If your check reveals something amiss – even slightly – spend a few moments exploring what would be needed to restore your baseline state of well-being. *Respect any information you receive,* and act on it fast.

Using imagery to activate your immune system

Many people have found that healthful and healing processes can be 'switched on' or focused through the use of imagery. Given the way in which we translate ideas and images into body experiences and vice versa, it's easy to use your Inner Coaching time to discover what images naturally seem to represent health, well-being and your own immune system itself. Take your immune system. It's absolutely crucial to your survival, but how much attention have you given it? You could start right now.

▶ Become inquisitive and receptive: what ideas, images or feelings come into your mind when you think about your immune system? We have known people who think of it as an internal police force, as an army of workmen and as a flock of voraciously hungry sheep. What's yours like when it's working well? And what helps it work well?

▶ Next time you or someone close to you is ill with a viral infection, use this knowledge to check that your immune system is functioning at its best. If it is not, ask yourself what adjustments you need to make. Is it sluggish, off-duty, overloaded or already occupied with something else? Follow up the answers you get: make adjustments to the images, if needed, and change actual behaviour (by taking a rest, for example).

▶ If you receive an injury, take inner time to pay attention to how it feels and looks, and to compare this with how it was before and how it will need to change in order for you to regain health. Then spend time intently concentrating on the process of changing from one to the other. We have worked with many clients over the years on health issues, and have shared their delight and surprise at how appropriate and successful their Inner Coaching interventions have been.

Becoming sensitive to what else affects your health

Sometimes when you become attentive in this way, you'll find yourself gaining information that at first seems to bear little relation to the health issue you began with. For example, you might find yourself thinking of difficulties at work, problems in a relationship or issues from the past that you find difficult to let go.

▶ Be willing to accept that a connection might exist between these issues and your current state of health. Take Inner Coaching time to invite your unconscious to search for relevant information and connections, and continue exploring until you find out more.

The more you do this, the greater will be your trust in your ability to make a difference when you really need to. As you use Inner Coaching to build this connectedness and work with your mind, body and spirit, you are creating a virtuous circle: the partnership you are building could be the source of your health 'miracle' if you should ever need one. Though, as we've shown, when it happens it won't actually be a miracle, but rather the result of your own work within yourself.

Deciphering dreams

Dreams can be one of the most exotic fruits of your unconscious processing. Everyone dreams every night – five or six times. Often, we don't remember our dreams when we wake, and some people almost never recall anything; but when we do, the images a dream presents or the feelings it evokes can linger all day. Some dreams, in fact, seem much more significant than others in what they touch off in us.

There have been many theories about dreams, and many different formulas for working with them to extract meaning. Trying to use dreams as tools of divination seems to be almost as old as human culture. More recently, Freud and then Jung offered models which are still being used today. However, we think you'll find the recent pioneering work of the psychologist Joseph Griffin particularly valuable. Griffin's model is well researched and thoroughly grounded in neurophysiology, and it has great explanatory power.

Briefly, it suggests that REM sleep enables us to deal with any emotionally arousing events of the day that remain unresolved. By playing out any 'unfinished business' to its conclusion via metaphoric images, dreaming deactivates the emotion and leaves the brain rested and ready to handle the next day's emotionally arousing onslaught. Dreams and the sleep that gives rise to them are thus essential to psychic health. Hence Shakespeare's view, in *Macbeth*, of:

Sleep that knits up the ravelled sleeve of care,
The death of each day's life, sore labour's bath,

> *Balm of hurt minds, great nature's second course,*
> *Chief nourisher in life's feast.*

In Elizabethan feasts the 'second course' was the meat course, hence 'Chief nourisher'. That's how important sleep is. And Macbeth, who can't sleep because he has murdered the King, knows this to his bitter cost.

The idea that dreams are a way to process emotionally arousing experiences has some interesting implications. When things are more charged *as far as you're concerned*, your dreams may be more vivid – not just about what occurred but often in anticipation of what may happen. (It's how much something matters to you, not the external magnitude of any event, that determines this.) Of course, if they are too charged you may be restless and feel like you're endlessly dreaming, or if things are very charged – say through fear or guilt – you may have trouble remaining asleep.

Griffin's approach also suggests to us that dreams testify to the power of meditation, particularly in aiding the release of accumulated stress. Ian can still recall the most vivid dreams he has ever had. They occurred when he was engaged in an intensive residential meditation retreat with 100 other people. The kind of meditation Ian does is Transcendental Meditation (TM). The TM model says that meditation enables a profound clearing out to occur. This will sometimes be experienced as stress release in the form of thinking, or fleeting emotions while meditating. When this is done in a group for many hours each day you really start cooking! And the dreams that happened at night made clear how much was being released. Yet from the outside all he had done was sit in a room with his eyes closed for much of the day.

Dream workshops, even dream books, can give you valuable pointers – so long as you remember that your dreams are a very individual creation. You won't find the meaning of your dreams by looking up symbols in a 'dream dictionary'! It makes more sense to assume that your dreams have personal significance for *you* than that they can reliably be interpreted in accordance with any standardised set of 'meanings'. It is better to reflect on the impact a dream had, and the way it reached you, than to try and translate it into a single coherent story. Jumps and dislocations are part of the very fabric of dreams.

Just paying your dreams some attention will start to create a better link between your conscious and unconscious. A more holistic awareness ensues where more of you is available to you more of the time. It's as if you're allowing one mode of consciousness to add savour to the other. If you want to engage with your dream world, consider the following when thinking about a dream you've had:

- What was the dominant feeling in the dream?

- What was the dominant feeling you were left with afterwards?

- Were any of the images particularly powerful, or recurrent?

- Was the dream itself an 'oft-told story' – one that repeats itself?

- Do you recognise bits and pieces of your recent experience, or issues that have recently concerned you?

- What was on your mind before from the day?

- Was anything preoccupying you or getting to you, be it nice or nasty, delightful or forbidden?

- Were there any feelings that have had no place to go or were not acknowledged by you during the day?

INNER COACHING EXERCISE: DREAM STATE

▶ Imagine yourself into your dream and allow it to continue . . .

▶ Or take on the role of the different objects and characters in turn and allow each to speak out its message . . .

▶ If something is bothering you, ask yourself at the end of your day if you could have a dream that would help you. Sometimes a request like this will be sufficient to allow you to dream such a dream there and then as your mindful state continues and deepens. Sometimes it will occur when you sleep the same night.

▶ If you are facing a decision, or wanting to develop some creative options for the future, ask if you might dream a dream that could help you benefit from your unconscious wisdom and your unconscious creativity.

Take what your dreams have to offer as an addition, not necessarily as a substitute. Be guided and enriched by your dreams, not governed by them.

Chapter Twelve

Everyday Gifts

Remember what we said earlier? That you are the most exciting, mysterious, complex, resourceful being in the known universe. If you've been doing the exercises and spending quality time with yourself, the explorations you have undertaken through your Inner Coaching will have begun to give you some inkling of what might be possible. Much of what we've been asking you to pay attention to may seem – on the face of it – quite 'ordinary' or 'everyday'. The trick is to recognise just how astonishing these everyday happenings and taken-for-granted abilities of yours are. Once you do, you enhance the possibility of utilising them to the full – and you increase your own self-appreciation and self-confidence at the same time.

Feeling good about yourself has a way of spreading and creating the kind of virtuous cycles we were talking about earlier. Feeling good means you have more confidence, explore more, try more, discover more, achieve more, feel better, explore more... And so on. It's also important because the more you become aware of how unique you are and exactly how you go about things, the more you can influence your-self. When you know how you work, you can play to your strengths and build your strengths where you need to. And, like all coaching, that empowers you at many levels.

Our experience is that these simple gifts are waiting for you if you learn to seek them and accept them. And as you get more into the habit of recognising, appreciating and enjoying these gifts to the full, so they will deepen your sense of harmony within yourself.

What kind of everyday gifts are we talking about? If you watch young children you'll notice that for the most part they:

- Are alert and interested in the world about them

- Are curious about new things and want to engage in new experiences

- Balance rest and activity

- Eat and sleep well

- Learn avidly

- Can be spontaneous and creative.

Children provide us with a useful template, and we'd like to take this as a kind of gold standard for the everyday gifts we're concerned with in this chapter. We believe that it's possible to count on these qualities and responses as a baseline for living. And when you do your regular self-monitoring in the way we suggested in the previous chapter, your Inner Coaching can let you know when things are not as they should be, and also help you find ways to regain your full well-being when you've been off-course.

We want to look more closely at some of these everyday gifts that make up a natural and rich experience of life. We'll also explore just how your Inner Coaching can help you regain and maintain them. It's easy to assume that using the word 'gifts' implies you're on the receiving end: we'd like you to be mindful of the fact that *you are also the giver*. To get the most out of what follows, consider as you read how you can be developing the kind of internal collaboration that makes this 'gift' of giving and receiving possible.

Being alert and interested

Being alert is your benchmark of being alive. At its most basic in wild animals, it is the difference between life or death. In human beings, being alert and interested is the difference between dying a slow death from boredom, emotional attrition and lack of opportunity to express their individual uniqueness – or seeking and finding experiences that enhance the life of their mind and spirit.

Paying attention to your inner experience will give you plenty of information about where you are on this continuum of possibilities. Do you find work, or other people, or even yourself, boring? Is a day just another day? Do the weeks, and perhaps even the years, slip past with little to show for them? Do you have to crank up your energy to do what needs to be done? Do you find yourself spending every evening slumped in front of the telly? These can all be signals from you to you – and they are ones to take seriously. Initially, you may find it easier to review the state of things through deliberate and regular periods of Inner Coaching. Then, as your self-monitoring becomes more practised and automatic, you'll find that you can access that special state for moments or even seconds to check out what you need.

If you had a number of 'yes' answers to the above questions, and find the prospect of making such changes alarming, look for small adjustments you can make, rather than huge ones that may be difficult or take time. For example, consider the attitude that you, and others, take towards life's ups and downs. Is it supportive, or limiting?

We know a young woman who had quite a tough childhood, yet she is always lively, enjoys being with other people and throws herself wholeheartedly into new learning and new experiences. When you ask her about the bad times, she tends to say, 'Yes, it was tough, but there's a gift in everything.' And when you enquire further, she can tell you what she learnt to see differently, approach in a new way and understand more fully about herself or others through those particular experiences.

Here's someone with a skill who knows how to keep a sense of proportion and put the past behind her when she chooses. Spending time with her makes you feel good, and her way of thinking tends to rub off on her friends. So you might also want to consider the company you keep.

INNER COACHING EXERCISE: DISCOVERING DELIGHT

▶ Think about people you know who seem to find life a delightful, enjoyable experience: watch them, talk to them, find out just how they do that – because finding life delightful can be a skill and a habit, not just the result of luck in what befalls you.

> ▶ Try their way of being on for size: imagine how they would have responded to something in your life which you found challenging, if it had happened to them.
>
> ▶ Wonder just how you could learn from them or emulate them.

INNER COACHING TIPS: LIVING LIFE TO THE FULL

> ▶ Use Inner Coaching to help you develop your own benchmarks for alertness by remembering times when you have felt really alive and interested. Reflect on exactly how and what you felt.
>
> ▶ Use these benchmarks to help you assess how alert you are feeling right now. Some people like to code things on a scale of one to ten. What number represents you at your most alert and alive? And where are you now? What would be your average for this month, or this year? Would you like it to be even higher?

Exploring and experimenting

Wanting to explore seems to happen naturally when you have enough energy – and are not frightened. Young children give us an obvious example: they can't wait to try new things out and discover what happens if ... Young animals are the same.

Wanting to explore and experiment is an indication of abundant vitality – and something that brings you in touch with new possibilities. This way you get to choose a life cram-full of living, rather than one that feels like you're just passing the time.

INNER COACHING EXERCISE: EXPLORATIONS

> ▶ In your neutral and welcoming inner space, remember the last time you were drawn to try out something new. Just what was it that engaged you?
>
> ▶ What kinds of ideas or experiences catch your interest? Begin wondering what these all have in common.

> ▶ Think about what you were really passionate about as a youngster. How did it feel to be that engaged, and that alive? Do you have a similar passion about anything now? If not, take some Inner Coaching time to wonder what that might be now.
>
> ▶ Is there anything you could get into, if only you gave yourself the chance? What would be a first step?

Balancing rest and activity

Young children and animals both respond to their bodies' needs easily and immediately. When they're alert they are really alert – and when they're tired they just flop. Social learning and physical maturing mean that we learn how to override these natural responses. You learn how to look interested even though you aren't, how to keep going through that after-lunch low, how to work long hours. You also learn how to make it difficult to go to sleep and how to wake early worrying ...

Learning to override what comes naturally has its uses; but it can also have drawbacks because you build a habit of denying your experience – sometimes even to yourself. And when overriding yourself becomes a habit, your mind and body start protesting. You could say that when you start to get divorced from yourself they often try to give you a wake-up call, be it with a physical symptom, a recurrent thought or a change in mood.

Conscious determination and unconscious organisation can work in tandem to help you with some of these things. Use your conscious mind to identify some things you could do, and access your unconscious wisdom through Inner Coaching to find alternatives you hadn't previously thought of and to help you set new patterns in place. Working with your varied resources like this is a great way to experience and reinforce your sense of wholeness and resourcefulness.

> ### INNER COACHING EXERCISE: FOLLOWING YOUR IN-BUILT RHYTHMS
>
> ▶ Remind yourself that a 1¹/₂-hour cycle of activity and rest (the ultradian cycle) occurs throughout the day. Think about how these peaks

and troughs occur in your daily life and how you could take advantage of them: stopping briefly for things like tea and coffee breaks; getting up, going out, walking around the building or the block; eating something nutritious and light rather than working right through your lunchtime with a snack at your desk; allowing yourself to stare out of the window or even to have a short doze as you take time just to be with yourself.

▶ Then ask your inner wisdom to allow you to respect and follow the fluctuations easily and naturally, so that without even thinking consciously about it you can get your life, and your energy, back in harmony.

How far you go is up to you. One stressed business executive we worked with decided he really needed to do something pretty radical. So come lunchtime each day he took his phone off the hook, switched off his mobile, put a do-not-disturb notice on his office door and stretched out on the floor for 20 minutes. After a week he felt less tired. After a month he not only felt alert and alive again but had also begun to benefit from what had been going on inside while he 'dozed'. Colleagues who had teased him at first began to notice his new energy. Ideas were flowing and his life both in business and at home was buzzing in a way it hadn't for a long time. 'I thought I couldn't afford to spare the time!' he said. 'How could I afford *not* to?'

When you are this alive and alert you're able to be more present in your life. This kind of all-over fitness allows you to become more flexible and elastic in your responses. In fact, flexibility is itself a sign of fitness, both in mind and body. Being all-over fit means you can respond more appropriately: your ability to concentrate improves, so you work better and enjoy your play more. You can enjoy slow time and manage fast time.

INNER COACHING TIPS: YOUR UPS AND DOWNS

Take some time to observe yourself, asking the following questions.

▶ When did you last enjoy some time when you didn't feel exhausted and could just take it easy?

> ▶ What happens when you're tired or losing focus but you feel under pressure to get something done? How do you feel and think – and what do you actually do?
>
> ▶ What kinds of signals do you get when your degree of alertness changes?
>
> ▶ Are there some signals you currently try to override?
>
> ▶ And what kinds of signals do you actually respond to?

Eating well

Food is fuel, fuel converts to energy and energy determines what you can and can't do. What's 'good' eating, then? When your diet and your needs are in alignment, you'll usually look forward to eating, and enjoy it. Eating well is usually followed by a sense of satisfaction and well-being as well as pleasure, and this is a useful litmus test. When you have a pattern of nutrition that works for you, you feel more energetic. You may initially lose weight and then stabilise. Or, as your energy levels increase, you may feel like taking more exercise and convert any flab into muscle. Take the time to check in with yourself when you feel hungry or thirsty, when you're buying food and deciding what to eat – and respect the answers you get. Over time, you may find your food preferences changing, perhaps a little, perhaps quite a lot.

INNER COACHING EXERCISE: FOOD FOR WELL-BEING

You can use your Inner Coaching to help you with these issues:

▶ Set yourself a task of unconscious self-monitoring to discover what kinds of food, drink and exercise enhance your fitness and well-being and what kinds detract from it.

▶ Ask your unconscious to bring any patterns or information that you need to know about (good and bad) into the forefront of your awareness so that you can take appropriate conscious action.

Sleep well

Good sleep is another everyday gift. When you have it, it is wholly unremarkable. Only when they don't have it do most people appreciate just what a gift it is. If you're getting enough sleep, you'll tend to wake feeling refreshed and alert, looking forward to a new day. Mostly, you'll fall asleep quite easily, and find it easy to drop off again if you wake during the night. However, many people are actually sleep deprived because they're not paying attention to their body's signals: they have become habituated to fatigue.

If you could trust yourself to wake up when you needed to, you'd be able to have quick naps when the opportunity arose. The vast majority of people have the ability to wake up within a minute or two of a pre-determined time – but they may not know that they have this gift or that they can 'set their personal alarm' to alert them after specific intervals.

INNER COACHING EXERCISE: TAKE IT EASY

▶ Give yourself a 20-minute break: set a kitchen timer for 25 minutes as a fail-safe, then just as you begin to take yourself into your Inner Coaching state, tell yourself *'I'd like to take 20 minutes.'* Use the time to rest profoundly, or to allow your unconscious to do some important inner work. For short intervals like this, most people will come to within a minute of the time they wanted to wake.

▶ Experiment with other time intervals and other purposes. For example, take yourself into your welcoming Inner Coaching space and set your internal timer to give yourself a ten-minute nap and wake up deeply refreshed. Many active people have naturally developed this ability – now you can emulate them. (However, don't be tempted to think that over time you can use these power-naps as a substitute for a good restful night's sleep. A long period of sleep allows for deeper healing processes to take place, and for your unconscious to process important material through dreaming.)

Anxiety and stress interfere with sleep, just as they do with appetite. There are times in everyone's life when this happens, and though it's inconvenient or even unpleasant, the normal pattern will usually reset itself once the disturbance or distress is past. Disruptions that continue may be a signal that you need to use your Inner Coaching to explore further. For example:

▶ If you always need an alarm to wake you, you're probably not getting enough sleep. Ask your unconscious to help you build a pattern of winding up the day sooner to ensure that you get the hours you really need.

▶ If you go to sleep, then wake after a couple of hours, or if you wake in the early hours of the morning and can't get back to sleep again, it's worth doing a little Inner Coaching on this.

▶ Go inside and ask yourself if, in your waking hours, you are trying to ignore things which might be causing tension, anxiety or sadness. Often we can mask such feelings reasonably effectively when we're awake, but they creep through when we're trying to rest. Poor sleep in these circumstances can be taken as a useful indicator that you need to take action.

INNER COACHING TIP: YOU AND YOUR HABITS

▶ When you think of yourself as someone who's got 'bad eating habits' or who is 'a poor sleeper', you are making an artificial separation between 'you' and your habits. And when you do that you do two things that keep you stuck: you block the signal that's seeking to reach you from within, and you place the real problem, whatever it may be, out of reach. So train yourself to notice when you think or speak like this, and to ask yourself, *'I wonder why I'm doing that?'* Repeat the question next time you do some Inner Coaching, and allow the difficulty to start a process of exploration that can lead you to an improvement at a deeper and more lasting level.

Learning avidly

Studies of people who live to a great age show that one of the things they have in common is that they continue to learn. They don't ever seem to think 'That's enough' or 'I'm too old now'. Learning is a natural way of being in the world, not an optional extra. In young children, it's about acquiring the information and skills that will give them influence over their environment. As we develop, learning becomes the key means by which we acquire influence over ourselves.

The drive to learn is inbuilt, so it will occur naturally unless it's interfered with. If avid learning and curiosity aren't a natural part of your life nowadays, it's worth asking yourself what happened to block them, and whether that's temporary or long-term.

Learning isn't just about acquiring external knowledge. Becoming more aware of what's going on inside yourself and others is learning, too. Learning literally involves growth and re-creation, because it involves making new neurological connections and pathways. People recognise this unconsciously when they say they feel 'stretched'.

Check out consciously with yourself:

- What is the learning you have most enjoyed?

- What are you learning nowadays?

- What's the learning you are most proud of?

INNER COACHING EXERCISE: LEARNING ABOUT LEARNING

Go within, and ask yourself:

▶ What makes it easy for you to learn?

▶ What makes it difficult, or blocks it?

▶ How would you like to take your learning forward?

Being spontaneous and creative

Creativity as we understand it is the ability to make new connections, to go beyond the habitual or the known – on your own terms, to behave in a new way, to think something new, to experiment and to explore.

Creativity and spontaneity can both arise when you're willing and open to allowing new connections to be made, rather than being quick to rule anything out on grounds of rationality, practicality or 'the done thing'. You can help encourage both creativity and spontaneity by building the habit of asking yourself, *'And what else?'* Don't run a totalitarian regime in your head! Seek to develop ease in the face of the unknown rather than fearing it. Get comfortable with difference and with the disturbance of familiar patterns.

Spontaneity emerges from a sense of trust in yourself. In our experience, the more you build the relationship with yourself through your Inner Coaching, the deeper that trust becomes. When you're spontaneous, you're responding quickly and naturally to what's going on inside and around you. You're not straitjacketing yourself with social censorship or being fearful about your vulnerability. You are able to be you. And you're not just doing the first thing that comes into your head, either. That's the kind of 'natural' behaviour that often backfires because it springs from an emotional reaction, not the kind of reflective inner coherence which comes with Inner Coaching.

By and large, the ability to act and respond spontaneously means that you have confidence in your ability to handle what comes next. It means you know you have influence, over yourself and others. It is what gives you the confidence to manage without having to be in control. Giving up the need to control doesn't mean 'going with the flow'. Having influence is rather like channelling the flow of water, steering a ship or riding a horse: it's about directing the path of energy, and working with its power rather than trying to dominate it, whether you're working with yourself or others.

Wendy has vivid memories of going to a grand college ball when she was an undergraduate. She knew it should be fun. The tickets cost a lot. But by the time the ball came around she and her then boyfriend were ready to split up, except that they had already paid for the tickets! So they duly went and grimly tried to enjoy themselves … That's what happens when you don't get creative and respond spontaneously.

INNER COACHING EXERCISE: BEING YOUR BEST

Use these questions as springboards for an Inner Coaching search. Sometimes it's good to consider these questions consciously, too, as this will round out the information you get.

▶ When have you felt most influential in your life? Find three examples. Looking back, consider how you were in yourself. What did you do and what did you not do to be so influential?

> ▶ Think of some times when you have not been spontaneous. Then think of some times when you were just impulsive. What lets you know the difference between them?
>
> ▶ What difference would it make in your life to be even more creative and spontaneous?

In this chapter we've explored some of your everyday gifts. They can greatly enrich your life, if only you let them. In a sense, we're asking you to get out of your own way, because the gifts are there for the enjoying. When people develop an authentic, regular and respectful communication with themselves this becomes easy to do. You can begin right now by developing a fuller appreciation of yourself using this next exercise.

INNER COACHING EXERCISE: YOUR SPECIAL GIFTS

> ▶ In your welcoming internal space, take some time to reflect on your own special gifts. What are they, and how could you use them more to enrich your life?

Postscript: Inner Coaching as a way of life

When you build rapport with yourself and become more fully receptive to information from within, you are building your fitness for life. Fitness in any sphere is a matter of regularity, because regular practice of any skill is what transforms a natural aptitude into a capability that you can rely on – and extend. It's the same with Inner Coaching. Just as athletes work out at the gym or follow specialised routines that build the kind of muscles and the type of stamina they need for their individual disciplines, when you make a habit of Inner Coaching you are building your fitness for whatever you encounter in life.

The importance of patterns and habits

Building your inner fitness doesn't require strenuous training. Rather, it's about establishing simple and regular patterns. You don't get to run a marathon for the first time by going out and trying to run ten miles. You may have to start by walking round the block. Every time you listen to what your intuition, your imagination, your dreams, and your body's messages are telling you, you're building that fitness – gradually and respectfully. Every time you ignore or dismiss these things, you're weakening yourself. When Inner Coaching becomes a natural daily occurrence rather than an irregular event, when you can consult yourself from moment to moment, anywhere, you enhance your effectiveness.

When you practise Inner Coaching as a personal discipline, you get even more from it, because you build greater refinement in understanding and utilising what all of your body-mind has to offer. You need to get to know your own uniqueness, so that you develop familiarity with your personal shorthand (*'When I get a migraine it's usually telling me that ... '*) and with how you work as a whole, which includes knowing your own range of preferred signalling systems. If you rarely remember your dreams, for example, a particular dream may have a stronger impact and more information for you than if you recall many of your dreams. You get to know what to take seriously, and what to take with a pinch of salt. You get to know which signals mean you need to take immediate action, and when to wait a while to see if the signal persists. You are getting to know you – and how to get the most from yourself.

These self-monitoring and self-correcting processes depend on you cultivating your relationship with yourself. Their essence is a free flow of information within you which allows you to develop a sense of what it means to be you, and to become alert both to what disturbs that personal equilibrium and what restores it. As with working out, the more you can do, the more you find you could do. You get to know where your frontiers of familiarity are, and to enjoy approaching and even crossing them. The more you know about travelling in your internal landscape, the more there is to discover.

To engage in regular Inner Coaching is to build a full relationship with yourself, one that, like any good relationship, is characterised by complexity and richness. It's one which includes – even welcomes – debate, difference, uncertainty, conflict and resolution as well as harmony. We're not aiming for a 'nice' relationship but one that's tough enough to wash and wear and stand up for a lifetime. Its uniqueness as an asset is that it gives you another take on your experience, and on yourself, and because your unconscious mind functions differently it makes different things possible. Your inner wisdom offers you *additional* ways of understanding and of being.

The lifelong benefits of Inner Coaching

Whatever the actual difficulties life throws at you – if you have a car crash or lose your job, or someone you love dies, for example – we'd say that what people generally find most difficult to manage is the *state* in which they find themselves. In particular, that means feeling overwhelmed, feeling scattered or feeling ungrounded. When you feel any of these, you feel less in control of yourself and your circumstances.

In fact, that's what really makes an emergency: not the event itself but the way it affects your state. That's why some people can remain effective even in a disaster. Training or their individual nature will have enabled them to maintain the state that's needed to respond appropriately. Their feelings may or may not be involved, but they aren't incapacitated by them.

Inner Coaching gives you an edge in dealing with emergencies, whether they're out-there events or inner upheavals, *just because it helps you recognise and manage the states they generate.* Even where you are initially thrown off balance by what's going on, Inner Coaching helps you rebalance more quickly. Using our fitness analogy, the key is your ability to recover, and how fast you can do it. If you watch a top athlete being interviewed after winning the 100 metres, he'll be breathing fast. But unlike most of us, he is capable of speech! He's fit enough, even immediately afterwards, to have the breath to talk. A few minutes later, his heart rate will be rapidly returning to normal again and his breathing rate will have slowed.

Mental and emotional fitness is much the same. It's natural to be shocked by the unexpected, to feel sad or helpless or confused or afraid. None of these feelings is incapacitating in itself. They're normal human responses, and the ability to experience them fully is an essential part of being fully alive. What's important is how fast you can regain your equilibrium. By this we mean your ability to act and react appropriately, whether or not you have left the feelings behind. Courage is the ability to act even while afraid – and achieving the level of fitness that allows you to be effective while upset, angry, puzzled, sad, excited or in the grip of other strong emotions depends on how much of you is available to help you.

The key to your personal fitness is how fast you can recognise your state and manage it.

One highly practical friend of ours was completely thrown one evening when she noticed smoke coming from under her bedroom door, and found her electric blanket had caught fire. She panicked. *'Water! Quick!'* she thought – and rushed for a tooth-mug. A moment or two later she came to her senses and realised what she was doing. The practical side of her kicked in again: despite the emergency she was able to laugh at herself – and then do something very different. She just threw the smouldering mattress out of the window. She recognised her state, she changed her state, then she could act effectively.

Doing more of what works

We've shown how Inner Coaching can act like a bridge from unresourceful states to more effective ones. And we've emphasised that this doesn't have to involve suppressing your feelings. What's important is developing your ability to feel and to act appropriately. Because it allows you to change state and gives you alternative perspectives from which to consider both your situation and your own part in it, Inner Coaching restores your ability to *choose* – and with renewed choice you once again have the possibility of influence and effectiveness.

Inner Coaching offers you exactly the same benefits when things are going well. You can identify just what's so enjoyable, personally enriching or successful about what's going on – so that you can enjoy it even more, prolong it or know how to do it again.

When you're enjoying something, when you're successful, it's great. But it can be better yet. There's a structure to your success, and a pattern to your enjoyment, which Inner Coaching can help you identify and repeat. You could experiment by entering a mindful state and asking yourself just *what* was so special, just *how* you went about creating that situation. For every piece of information you already know in consciousness, there will be others that you know unconsciously. Once brought into awareness, they come together to provide you with the means for living a fuller, freer life.

Many decisions we have to make in life are complex. Our conscious minds can weigh up more or less easily things which are relatively alike. But through Inner Coaching you have access to that part of you which can weigh up things that are not alike – and make wise decisions.

Our own lives have been immeasurably enriched by this process of Inner Coaching. We know yours can be too.

Resources - Where to Next?

If you have found this book of interest you might enjoy actually working with a coach who is trained in this particular way of working. With coaching now the flavour of the month we urge you to be very careful and check out people's credentials. At the present time it is very much a case of buyer, beware. To be sure of finding someone suitable we suggest you contact us.

You can contact Wendy Jago via email: wendyandleo.jago@virgin.net or, for corporate coaching, training or consultancy, via Designer Learning, +44 (0)1594 560975.

You can contact Ian McDermott and get further information via his website: www.itsnlp.com.

Free Updates

If you would like to receive free updates on new material and relevant trainings you can contact us by post or email.

International Teaching Seminars
ITS House
Webster Court
Websters Way
Rayleigh
Essex
SS6 8JQ
Tel: +44 (0)1268 777125   Fax: +44 (0)1268 777976

Or just go to the website www.itsnlp.com and give us your email address.

Further Reading

There are an extraordinary number of books which could be of interest. However, we believe these ones will give you a lot of practical guidance in engaging with more of yourself.

Connirae Andreas & Steve Andreas, *Heart of the Mind*, Real People Press, 1990

Deepak Chopra, *Quantum Healing: Exploring the Frontiers of Mind/Body Medicine*, Bantam, 1989

Guy Claxton, *Hare Brain, Tortoise Mind*, Fourth Estate, 1997

Robert Dilts, Tim Hallbom & Suzi Smith, *Beliefs: Pathways to Health & Wellbeing*, Metamorphous Press, 1990

W. Timothy Gallwey, *The Inner Game of Tennis*, Random House, 1974

Joseph Griffin, *The Origin of Dreams*, Human Givens Publishing Ltd., 1997

Nancy Kline, *Time to Think*, Cassell Illustrated, 1998

Ian McDermott & Joseph O'Connor, *NLP and Health*, HarperCollins, 1996

Ian McDermott and Wendy Jago, *The NLP Coach*, Piatkus, 2001

Ernest Rossi, *The 20 Minute Break*, Zeig, Tucker & Theisen Inc., 1991

Ernest Rossi, *The Psychobiology of Mind-Body Healing*, W. W. Norton, 1986

Joseph E. Shorr, *Go See the Movie in Your Head*, Atlantic Books, 1984

Index

Note: page numbers in **bold** refer to diagrams.